# EVERYTHING YOU NEED TO KNOW ABOUT
# SOCCER!

**THIRD EDITION**
**Senior Editor** Rona Skene
**Senior US Editor** Megan Douglass
**Art Editor** Chrissy Barnard
**Consultant** Tracey Bourne FHEA, MA, UEFA B
(FA Tutor, Sporting (Football) Excellence & Sport Coaching
Apprenticeships Assessor)
**Managing Editor** Francesca Baines
**Managing Art Editor** Philip Letsu
**Production Editor** Jacqueline Street-Elkayam
**Senior Production Controller** Jude Crozier
**Senior Jacket Designer** Akiko Kato
**Senior DTP Designer** Harish Aggarwal
**Senior Jackets Coordinator** Priyanka Sharma Saddi

**FIRST EDITION**
**Senior Editor** Chris Hawkes
**Senior Art Editors** Mik Gates, Stefan Podhorodecki
**Editor** Suhel Ahmed
**Designers** David Ball, Chrissy Barnard,
Kit Lane, Simon Mumford, Sadie Thomas
**Illustrations** Adam Benton, Stuart Jackson-Carter,
Jon@kja-artists
**Creative Retouching** Steve Crozier
**Picture Research** Nic Dean, Surya Sarangi
**Senior Jacket Designer** Mark Cavanagh
**Jacket Designers** Tanya Mehrotra, Suhita Dharamjit
**Jacket Editor** Claire Gell
**Jackets Editorial Coordinator** Priyanka Sharma
**DTP Designer** Rakesh Kumar
**Managing Jackets Editor** Saloni Singh
**Jacket Design Development Manager** Sophia MTT
**Consultant** Tracey Bourne (Football Studies—
Southampton Solent University; FA Associate tutor)
**Producer (Preproduction)** Jacqueline Street
**Senior Producer** Gary Batchelor
**Managing Art Editor** Philip Letsu
**Managing Editor** Francesca Baines
**Publisher** Andrew Macintyre
**Art Director** Karen Self
**Associate Publishing Director** Liz Wheeler
**Publishing Director** Jonathan Metcalf

This American Edition, 2022
First American Edition, 2017
Published in the United States by DK Publishing
1745 Broadway, 20th Floor, New York, NY 10019

Copyright © 2017, 2020, 2022 Dorling Kindersley Limited
DK, a Division of Penguin Random House LLC
22 23 24 25 26 10 9 8 7 6 5 4 3 2 1
001–332749–Sep/2022

DK books are available at special discounts when purchased in bulk
for sales promotions, premiums, fund-raising, or educational use. For
details, contact: DK Publishing Special Markets, 1745 Broadway,
20th Floor, New York, NY 10019
SpecialSales@dk.com

Printed and bound in China

For the curious
www.dk.com

**MIX**
Paper | Supporting
responsible forestry
FSC™ C018179

This book was made with Forest Stewardship Council ™
certified paper – one small step in DK's commitment to
a sustainable future. For more information go to
www.dk.com/our-green-pledge

# CONTENTS

## The beautiful game

## Play to the whistle

## A team game

## Tournaments and trophies

## Individual skills

# The beautiful game

No one knows who invented soccer. However, once the game's rules were set down in 1863, it did not take long for soccer to reach every corner of the world. Today, it is the most popular sport on the planet, with around 5 billion fans.

# Ancient ball games

Humans have been playing ball games **for at least 4,000 years**. Each of these early games had their **own rules**, some of which are **similar to soccer**.

People of all social classes played cuju, which was popular for many centuries.

Cuju, meaning "kick ball," was also played in Japan, Korea, and Vietnam.

Cuju was first played in China over 2,000 years ago, and it shares many similarities with modern soccer. Players could not use their hands or arms, and points were scored by kicking the ball into a goal.

## MESOAMERICAN BALL GAME

Played in Central America 3,600 years ago, the Mesoamerican ball game is the world's oldest team sport. Players played on a court, could not use their hands, and scored goals by getting the ball to go through a hoop.

**A competitive game** consisted of two teams of 12–16 players on each side.

**Individual players** attracted fame and fortune, and, by the 10th century, there was even a national championship to decide the best team.

**The ball** had an outer covering made of leather and was stuffed tightly with feathers.

# Birth of soccer

A variety of soccerlike games were played in **English boarding schools** in the **mid-19th century**. However, **the rules** of these games were **so different**, that it was virtually impossible for the school teams to play against each other.

**Eight players** make up the bully: 3 "corners," 2 "sideposts," 1 "post," 1 "pup," and 1 "fly."

**Players outside the bully are called "behinds."** Their role is to kick the ball over the bully toward the opponent's goal.

**Behinds** are made up of two types of player: "shorts" and "longs."

The rules for the **Eton Field Game** were first written down in 1815.

## THE FOOTBALL ASSOCIATION (FA)

Englishman Ebenezer Morley could be called the father of the Football Association. His letter, suggesting that soccer should have a common set of rules (meaning that teams could play against each other), led to a series of meetings that ended with the foundation of the Football Association on October 26, 1863. The game's first set of rules were published a few months later.

At the school of Eton, they played—and still do—the "Field Game." As in soccer, the ball is round and players are not allowed to pick up. However, the rules are more complicated than in soccer, and there is also a scrum, called a "bully."

## FIRST INTERNATIONAL

The first international was played between England and Scotland in Glasgow, Scotland, in 1872. It finished 0–0.

**Soccer spread to countries through the many connections** of the British Empire, introduced by the huge number of British workers who traveled throughout the world. It did not take long before these countries started to form their own national associations.

**1863** The Football Association, soccer's first national governing body, is established in England.

**1876** The Welsh FA is founded.

**1891** New Zealand becomes the first country outside Europe to create a national association.

**1893** The first national association in South America is established in Argentina.

**1904** The Haiti Football association is formed—the first in North America.

**1921** Egypt becomes the first African country to create a national association.

**1924** The Chinese Football Association is founded.

**1928** Israel and Palestine both create national associations.

# 1860

**1873** Scotland forms the world's second national association.

# 1890

**1889** Denmark and the Netherlands become the first countries on continental Europe to create national associations.

**1912** The Canadian Soccer Association is founded. The US Soccer Federation follows a year later.

# 1920

**1939** By the start of World War II, there were 109 national associations.

# Soccer spreads around the world

Established in 1857, **Sheffield FC** is the **world's** oldest soccer club.

After the Football Association was established in England in 1863, it took **little more than a century** for soccer to appear on **every continent** and in **virtually every country** in the world.

**1947** A national association is created in newly formed Pakistan.

**1965** The Zimbabwe Football Association is formed after the country gains its independence from Britain.

**1971** The United Arab Emirates Football Association is formed in the same year the country is created.

**1989** Belarus becomes the first former Soviet state to form its own national association.

**2016** Both Kosovo and Gibraltar become members of FIFA.

**1950**

**1980**

**1960** Twelve national associations are formed around the world; the most in a single year.

**1961** Football Federation Australia is formed, 70 years after its equivalent in New Zealand.

**1991** The South African Football Association is reformed following the end of apartheid.

# The modern era

The **Fédération Internationale de Football Association (FIFA)** is the game's international governing body. **Every continent**, with the exception of Antarctica, **has its own confederation**, which organizes international and club competitions.

## CONCACAF

CONCACAF governs the game in North and Central America and the Caribbean. Its headquarters are in Miami, Florida.

**Formed:** 1961
**Members:** 41
**Men's tournaments:**
*International*
CONCACAF Gold Cup
*Club*: CONCACAF Champions League
**Women's tournament:**
CONCACAF W Championship

## UEFA

UEFA is the governing body of soccer in Europe. Its headquarters are located in Nyon, Switzerland.

**Formed:** 1954
**Members:** 55
**Men's tournaments:**
*International*:
UEFA European Championship;
*Club*: UEFA Champions League,
UEFA Europa League
**Women's tournaments:**
UEFA Women's Euro,
UEFA Champions League

## CONMEBOL

The oldest of the continental confederations, CONMEBOL governs soccer in South America and its headquarters are in Luque, Paraguay.

**Formed:** 1916
**Members:** 10
**Men's tournaments:**
*International*: Copa América
*Club*: Copa Libertadores, Copa Sudamericana
**Women's tournaments:**
Copa América Femenina, Copa Libertadores Femenina

## CAF

The CAF governs soccer in Africa. Its HQ is in Cairo, Egypt.

**Formed:** 1957
**Members:** 54
**Men's tournaments:**
*International*:
Africa Cup of Nations
*Club*: CAF Champions League, CAF Confederation Cup
**Women's tournaments:**
Africa Women Cup of Nations, CAF Women's Champions League

## FIFA

FIFA is soccer's global governing body. Its headquarters are in Zurich, Switzerland.

**Formed:** 1904
**Members:** 211
**Men's tournaments:**
FIFA World Cup, FIFA Confederations Cup, Olympic Games
**Women's tournaments:**
FIFA Women's World Cup, Olympic Games

## AFC

The AFC governs soccer in Asia and Australia from its headquarters in Kuala Lumpur, Malaysia.

**Formed:** 1954
**Members:** 47
**Major tournaments:**
*International*: AFC Asian Cup
*Club*: AFC Champions League, AFC Cup
**Women's tournaments:**
AFC Women's Asian Cup, AFC Women's Club Championship

FIFA's motto is: "For the game. For the world."

## OFC

Founded in 1966, the OFC governs the game in Oceania from its HQ in Auckland, New Zealand.

**Formed:** 1966
**Members:** 11
**Major tournaments:**
*International*: OFC Nations Cup
*Club*: Oceania Club Championship
**Women's tournament:**
OFC Women's Nations Cup

## CUT OFF IN ITS PRIME

By 1920, the women's game was as popular as the men's, with one game in England featuring Dick, Kerr's Ladies (above, right), attracting a crowd of 53,000. In 1921, however, the FA banned women's games at their fields, saying the sport was inappropriate for women.

**1881** An unofficial women's international game is played between Scotland and England in Edinburgh on May 7, 1881. Scotland win 3–0.

**1921** The Football Association bans women's teams from playing on association member's fields.

**1890s** Several women's clubs are formed in England. One game, in north London, attracted a crowd of 10,000.

**1930s** Women's leagues are established in France and Italy.

 **1881**

**1930**

**1919** The first-ever women's French Championship is played—only two teams take part.

**1920** Dick, Kerr's Ladies, England's leading women's team, play a French XI in France. They win the game 2–0, in front of a crowd of 62,000

# Women's soccer

**Action from the 2015 FIFA Women's World Cup** game between the Ivory Coast and Thailand (which Thailand won 3–2). The tournament, held in Canada, featured 24 teams for the first time and was shown on television in 171 countries.

**Women's soccer** has gone through many **ups and downs** over the years. Once as popular as the men's game, it was then **banned**, but it has enjoyed a **huge resurgence** in recent times.

**1951** The first women's league is established in the United States.

**1971** The FA lifts its ban on women's soccer. The same year, UEFA recommends the women's game should be taken under the control of the national associations of each country.

**1984** Sweden wins the first official UEFA Women's European Championship.

**1996** Women's soccer is included in the program of events at the Olympic Games for the first time.

**2017** The number of national women's teams participating in international games rises to 176.

## 1960

## 1980

**1969** A group of women's clubs form the Women's FA in England.

**1989** Japan becomes the first country to launch a semi-professional women's league.

**1991** The United States wins the first FIFA Women's World Cup.

**1957** Germany organizes an unofficial women's European Championship.

The first FIFA-approved women's international was played in 1971.

# Overtime

The **10 essentials** of the ancient Chinese game of **cuju** included: respect for other players, courtesy, *team spirit*, no ungentlemanly behavior, **no dangerous play, and no ball-hogging.**

Balls in the **Mesoamerican ball game** from Central America varied; some were as small as **tennis balls,** while others could weigh up to 8 lb (3.6 kg)—that's the same weight as a **watermelon**.

**73 percent** of FIFA member associations have a **senior women's team.**

**30 million** women and **girls** around the world play soccer.

## Countries with the most registered players

If a player plays for a club, they are normally registered with their national football or soccer association. The graphic below shows the countries with the most registered players (female and male).

**United States**
1
1.7 million

**Canada**
2
300,000

**Germany**
3
203,000

**Female players**

**Germany**
1
5.9 million

**United States**
2
2.5 million

**Brazil**
3
2.1 million

**Male players**

# The world's richest leagues

Leagues make the majority of their money by selling the rights to show games to television companies. The world's top-five richest leagues are all in Europe, with England's Premier League at the top.

**Premier League England**
$6.9 billion

**Bundesliga Germany**
$3.4 billion

**Ligue 1 France**
$1.9 billion

**Serie A Italy**
$2.6 billion

**La Liga Spain**
$3.9 billion

# 50 percent

of FIFA member association countries have a **youth team.**

FIFA **has** 211 **members**, **compared with the** United Nation's 193.

# Countries with the most **professional male** players

According to a FIFA report in 2019, the country with the highest number of registered professional soccer players is Mexico.

**Mexico**
9,753

**Brazil**
9,177

**England**
5,935

**Argentina**
3,920

**Turkey**
3,693

# Play to the whistle

Anyone can play soccer: all you need is a ball and a space to play. Even the professional game is relatively simple: two teams of 11 players play for 90 minutes, while the game officials (the referee and the assistant referees) ensure that both teams play to the Laws of the Game.

# Laws of the game

Soccer has **17 laws** that cover every aspect of the game. The **English FA** devised 13 of these in **1863**. The remaining four were added later on.

**5** The referee
The appointed referee, whose decisions are final, is in charge of the game.

**6** Other match officials
Two assistant referees and other match officials, including video match officials, assist the referee to control the match.

**7** Game duration
A match is played over two periods of 45 minutes each, with a break at half-time.

**1** Field of play
The field size may vary, but must be rectangle, with the correct markings.

**2** The ball
The ball must weigh 14–16 oz (410–450 g) and be about 8⅔ in (22 cm) in diameter.

**3** Number of players
A team has 11 players. A game cannot take place with fewer than seven players in a team.

**4** Players' equipment
Players must wear a shirt with sleeves, shorts, socks, shin protectors, and soccer cleats.

5. The referee

1. Field of play

1863
1891
1902

3. Number of players

The original "Laws of the Game" were handwritten by Ebenezer Cobb Morley in 1863.

**8 Start/restart of play**
A kick off starts play, and restarts the game after a goal.

**9 Ball in play**
The ball is always in play unless the referee stops the game.

**10 Method of scoring**
A goal is scored when the whole ball crosses the line of the goal.

**11 Offside**
A player may be offside if they gain an advantage from having any part of the head, body, or feet nearer to the opponents' goal-line than both the ball and the last defender.

**12 Fouls and misconduct**
Players must play the game fairly and safely, and will be penalized for any unfair or unsporting behavior.

**13 Free kick**
A team wins a free kick for any foul or offense committed against them. It is taken from the spot where the offense occurred.

**14 Penalty kick**
A team may be awarded a penalty kick for a foul committed by an opponent in the opposition's penalty area.

**15 Throw-in**
A team wins a throw-in when the ball crosses the touchline after touching an opposition player last.

**16 Goal kick**
The defending team wins a goal kick if the ball crosses their own goal line after touching an opposition player last.

**17 Corner kick**
The attacking team wins a corner if an opposition player touches the ball last before it crosses the goal line.

12. Fouls and misconduct

10. Method of scoring

15. Throw-in

17. Corner kick

**The first fields had no markings**. Flags were used to mark the corners. The goalposts were set 8 yards (7.32 m) apart—the same as today—but had no crossbar.

**Two 6-yard (5.5-m) semicircles** were placed in front of the goal. Players could not touch the goalkeeper in these areas.

1863

**FIELD SIZE** 200 yards (180 m) long, 100 yards (90 m) wide

1891

**An 18-yard (16.4-m) line** was added to denote the penalty area.

**FIELD SIZE** 200 yards (180 m) long, 100 yards (90 m) wide

1937

**In 1882, field markings** were added. Following the introduction of the penalty kick in 1891, a 12-yard (10.9-m) line was marked across the field. A player could take a penalty from anywhere along the line.

Natural grass

Artificial fiber

**Hybrid grass**—a mix of natural and artificial grass— is the surface most clubs use today. Artificial fibers are injected 7.9 in (20 cm) deep into the soil and cover around 3 percent of the playing surface.

# The field

## The FA's first rulebook contained no guidelines for field markings, and it was only in the early 20th century that soccer fields began to take their modern form.

**A tape** was first hung between the goalposts in 1872. It was positioned 8 ft (2.4 m) above the ground. A solid crossbar replaced it in 1875.

**The 18-yard (16.4-m) line** was shrunk in 1902 to become the penalty area. The D, or arc, of the penalty area was added in 1937 to ensure that players were at least 10 yards (9 m) from the penalty spot when a player took a penalty.

FIELD SIZE 100–120 yards (90–120 m) long, 50–100 yards (45–90 m) wide

The **average field** contains an average of **300 million** blades of grass.

**The size and appearance of a soccer field** have changed dramatically since the game was first played in 1863. The illustrations above show how field markings have changed over the years.

### UNDER-SOIL HEATING

Most clubs have under-soil heating systems beneath the playing surface. These consist of hundreds of yards of tubes that contain hot water pipes that prevent the field from freezing over during winter.

# The soccer ball

The **earliest soccer balls** were **inflated pig bladders** covered with leather. Ball technology has changed dramatically over the years, both in terms of **how balls are manufactured** and **what they are made of**.

**Medieval soccer players** used a leather ball stuffed with an inflated pig's bladder, but this did not bounce well and often deflated. The modern ball has an outer cover made of synthetic leather, an inner lining to make it bouncy, and an inflated rubber bladder in the center.

**The oldest-known soccer ball** was found in a Scottish castle. When analyzed, it dated back to the 1540s.

1970s "Buckyball"

1990s ball

**The buckyball** consists of 20 hexagonal and 12 pentagonal panels stitched together.

1880s ball

1850s ball

Oldest-known soccer ball

## FAST FACTS

**Soccer balls** come in a range of standard sizes depending on the type of soccer being played and the age of the players.

Age: 14+

**Size 5 ball**
27–28 in
(68.5–71 cm)

Age: Under 14

**Size 4 ball**
25–26 in
(63.5–66 cm)

Age: Under 10

**Size 3 ball**
23–24 in
(58.5–61 cm)

**Beach soccer ball**
27–28 in
(68.5–71 cm)

**There are three main components** of a modern ball: the outer cover, the inner lining, and the bladder.

**Most bladders** contain pressurized air. Indoor soccer balls contain foam to reduce bounce.

**The inner lining** gives the ball its strength and bounce.

**Modern outer covers** are made of synthetic leathers such as polyvinyl chloride (PVC).

5 PRO QUALITY GRASS

INFLATE TO 10-12 PSI/ 0.70-0.84 BAR — DO NOT OVER INFLATE

ALPHA GLIDE
SuperSeam
OFFICIAL MATCH BALL

Circumference: 27–28 in (68.5–71 cm)

Modern-day soccer ball

**Thermal bonding** has replaced stitching in modern balls. Panels are placed into a mold and are stuck together by heat.

More than **40 million** soccer balls are produced each year.

# Geared up

**Soccer uniforms** have changed dramatically over the years, from the **thick cotton shirts** and **baggy shorts** of the 19th century, to the **high tech materials** used to make today's.

**HOME AND AWAY UNIFORMS**

In 1921, the law was changed so that, in the event of a color clash, the away team (and not the home team) had to change. Nowadays, all teams have a home uniform and an away uniform, with some teams also having a third uniform.

**Modern shirts** are normally made of a polyester mesh that does not trap in heat or sweat. They also contain lycra, which adds strength and flexibility.

**Sleeves** can either be long or short according to the Laws of the Game.

**Soccer uniforms** are used to distinguish between the two teams when they are on the field. Their design has changed hugely over the years. This illustration compares an 1890s uniform to one worn by players today.

**Early soccer shirts** were made of thick cotton and had collars. Some team's shirts were even made of wool!

**Team uniforms** started to emerge in the 1870s.

**Modern shorts** are loose, which allows for freedom of movement and good air circulation.

**Future shirts could contain computers that monitor a player's heart rate.**

**Modern shin pads** are made of many different synthetic materials. They are designed to spread the load of any impact over as wide an area as possible.

**Socks** must entirely cover the shin guard.

**Today**

**1890**

**Shorts** had to cover the knees according to a Football Association rule passed in 1904.

**The first player to wear shin guards** was Nottingham Forest's Sam Weller Widdowson in 1874. He wore a pair of cut-down cricket pads strapped to the outside of his socks.

**Socks** worn by early players could be any color. Clubs were not required to register the color and design of their socks until 1937.

# Perfect cleats

Early soccer cleats were designed to provide players with **both protection** and **grip on the field**. Nowadays, following years of development, the main function of the modern cleat is to **improve a player's performance**.

**The cleat's surface** contains ridges of varying sizes. These are designed to aid touch and ball control.

**The upper part of the cleat** is flexible, which helps the player's movement.

**Studs** have been shaped like arrows. Tests show that this shape provides better grip.

**Modern cleats** are a product of detailed research into comfort, a player's movement, and which part of the foot comes into contact with the ball the most.

**An elasticized, knitted collar** aids movement, ensures the cleat is more firmly attached to the foot, and is comfortable.

## EARLY CLEATS

Early soccer cleats were made of leather, and were uncomfortable and heavy. It was not until 1891 that the Football Association allowed cleats to be fitted with studs.

**The cleat's sole** is shaped to fit the foot perfectly.

The **earliest-known soccer cleats** were worn by **English king Henry VIII** in 1526.

**The cleat's plastic sole** is flexible to increase a player's mobility.

**The position of the studs** has been established after detailed research into a player's movement on the field.

**Top-flight referees** carry hi-tech equipment worth thousands of dollars onto the pitch. In addition, the goal-line technology system costs hundreds of thousands of dollars to install and maintain in a stadium.

**A headset** is used by the referee to communicate with the assistant referees. It is designed to ensure that they can hear one another clearly—even inside a noisy stadium.

**The red and yellow cards** are usually kept inside a wallet, which also contains a notepad for the referee to record incidents that occur during a game.

**A two-way radio receiver** relays the messages from the headset. The radio is powered by a battery pack.

Before whistles, referees used **handkerchiefs** to draw the attention of players.

**The goal-line technology (GLT)** wrist device is linked to a computerized camera system, which monitors both goals, and alerts the referee if the ball fully crosses either goal line.

# The referee

The referee is responsible for **enforcing** the **Laws of the Game**. At elite level, referees are equipped with **state-of-the-art technology** to help them with their job.

**The signal beep system** buzzes and vibrates whenever either assistant referee presses a button on their flags. This alerts the referee to any infringement.

**A stopwatch** is used to keep track of the game time. At elite level, the watch also includes a heart rate monitor to measure the referee's fitness level.

**A whistle** is used to signal the start and restart the game, stop play due to a foul or injury, and to end each half.

## MARKER SPRAYS

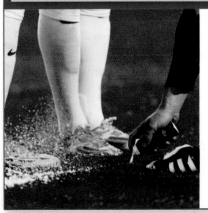

When a team is awarded a free kick, the referee uses a foaming spray to create a temporary marker 10 yards (9.1 m) away from the kick. The defenders must stand behind the mark at the moment the free kick is taken.

# Assistant referees

**Assistant referees** help the referee **enforce the Laws of the Game.** One assistant referee runs along each touchline and is responsible for half of the pitch. **The referee may overrule a decision made by an assistant referee.**

**An assistant referee communicates** with the referee via a small radio set.

**Assistant referees** officiate in situations in which the referee is not ideally positioned to see an incident and make the best decision.

**A button on the flag** is used to alert the referee instantly of any decision. This sends a beeping or vibrating signal to the referee.

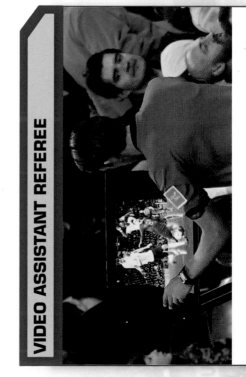

**VIDEO ASSISTANT REFEREE**

If necessary, referees can review major incidents (red cards, goals, and penalty decisions) using pitch-side video assistant referee (VAR) technology.

Assistant referees were known as linesmen before 1996.

**The flag** is brightly colored to ensure maximum visibility when the assistant referee makes a signal.

FAST FACTS

## The Diagonal System

is the most common method used by referees to officiate in a game. The referee (R) patrols a diagonal line that runs from the opposite corners of each penalty area. Each assistant referee (AR) is responsible for a separate half of the field.

**Assistant referees** use a set of standard flag signals to alert the referee to incidents and infringements that occur in their half of the field.

### Substitution

A flag is held above the head with both hands to indicate a team's wish to make a substitution.

### Offside

The flag is held above the head to signal for an offside offense.

### Throw-in

A flag is held out to one side, pointing in the direction of play of the team awarded the throw-in.

**3 hours**

**2 hours**

**1½ hours**

**1** Teams arrive
Players make their way to the stadium up to three hours before kick off. The away team arrives on the team bus.

**2** Team announcement
Both managers reveal their team's starting lineup and the list of substitutes to the press.

**3** Focusing the mind
Players begin their mental preparation. They each have their own ritual for staying relaxed and focused right up to kickoff.

In 2012, GSP Polet's Vuk Bakic scored **directly from a kickoff** in a Serbian league game.

# Countdown to **kickoff**

Before the **game** kicks off, the players spend up to **two hours** preparing for the **physical** and **mental** challenges of the game ahead.

**45 min**

**15 min**

**5 min**

**4 Warm-up**
Players take part in low-level exercise drills to warm up key muscle groups.

**5 Team talk**
The team gathers in the locker room for a final pep talk. The referee asks the teams to line up in the tunnel five minutes before kickoff.

**6 Sporting gesture**
The two teams run onto the field and shake hands. The players then take their position on the field.

**7 Kickoff**
A coin toss decides which team kicks off from the center circle. The referee blows the whistle and the game gets underway.

# Caught offside

An **attacker** is in an **offside position** if they are closer to the **opponent's goal** than any of the **defenders** when the ball is **kicked to the player**. The rule stops attackers from **hanging** out near the goal.

**Although this player** is in an offside position, it is not an offside infringement because the player is not active in play.

## ACTIVE IN PLAY

A player can only be offside if he or she receives the ball in the opposition's half of the field. The player must also be active in the play, or be giving the team an advantage by being in that position.

**In this game scenario**, the attacking player passes the ball to a teammate who is in an offside position. The team is immediately penalized and the opposition wins an indirect free kick.

An attacker is **not offside** if he or she **receives the ball from a corner, throw-in,** or **goal kick.**

**Player A** stays onside, as he is level with the defender closest to the goal line.

**2. Player B** is offside. When he receives the pass and becomes active in play, he is closer to the opposition goal than any of the defenders.

**3. The assistant referee** stands in line with the defender closest to the goal. The official raises the flag to signal that an attacking player is offside.

Ⓐ

Ⓑ

**The line of offside** is based on the position of the defender who is closest to the team's goal line.

**4. The referee** spots the assistant referee's offside signal and stops play. The defending team will be awarded an indirect free kick.

**1. The attacker** puts the team in a potentially offside position by passing the ball to player B. He should have passed to player A.

## 📈 FAST FACTS

**Originally, the offside rule** forced attackers to stay in front of two defenders. The rule was revised to a single defender in 1925, and led to a 36 percent increase in the number of goals scored across the English leagues during the following season.

1924–25 season

1925–26 season

4,700 goals     6,373 goals

# What is a **foul?**

The rules state that soccer must be played **fairly** and **safely**. It is the **referee's** job to call a **foul** if a player commits an **unfair act**, and to award the opposition a **free kick**—or a **penalty** if the foul occurred in the penalty box.

## FAST FACTS

Premier League, England **10**

La Ligue, France **11**

Bundesliga, Germany **11.5**

Serie A, Italy **13**

La Liga, Spain **13**

**The teams** in Europe's top five leagues commit between 10 and 13 fouls per game. The English Premier League records the lowest number. This is perhaps because the referees are more lenient.

## COMMON FOULS

A foul can be committed in a number of ways. Below are among the most common:

**Handball**
Intentional use of any part of the hand or arm to control the ball.

**Obstruction**
Blocking an opponent without making any attempt to play the ball.

**Tripping**
Intentionally tripping up an opponent.

**Holding**
Pulling on an opponent's shirt to slow them down.

**Dangerous play**
Making a reckless tackle that endangers a player's safety.

**The fouled player** stumbles over from the force of the reckless tackle.

**The tackler slides** in and makes contact with the opponent before touching the ball.

**Any tackle** that puts a player's safety at risk is a serious foul. This includes sliding in to make a challenge with the cleat studs raised.

Brazil committed **31 fouls** in a match versus Colombia at the FIFA 2014 World Cup!

# Free kicks

A team wins a **free kick** whenever the opposition commits a **foul** outside their own penalty area. The free kick is taken from the **spot** where the offense occurred and, if it is close to the opponent's goal, can present a good **goal-scoring** chance.

If a team shoots a free kick into its own goal, the opposition is awarded a corner.

Curving shot

The goalkeeper guards the area around the post closest to him.

## TYPES OF FREE KICK

Signal for a direct free kick

Signal for an indirect free kick

There are two types of free kick—direct and indirect. The referee awards a direct free kick against a foul, whereas an indirect free kick results from a technical infringement. Direct free kicks can be shot straight into goal, but an indirect free kick must be touched by a teammate first.

In this direct free kick, the player has a shot on goal. It is up to him to decide where to direct the shot, and then either drill, curve, spin, or apply dip to the ball.

## SHOOTING OPTIONS

↑ **Curving shot**
The free kick taker strikes across the ball with the side of the foot. This applies spin and makes the ball curve in the air.

↑ **Dipping shot**
In this type of free kick, the player puts top spin on the ball by striking it with the laces and then shortening the follow-through.

↑ **Through the wall**
The player shoots the ball low and fast underneath the wall. This may catch off-guard any defenders who jump up, expecting an aerial shot.

**The defensive wall** is made up of several players who stand in a line to guard the goal. They must be at least 10 yd (9 m) away from the ball.

Dipping shot

Curving shot

**The free kick taker** is a specialist who can direct the shot with pace and accuracy

**The top left-hand corner** of the goal is the natural side for the right-footed player to aim.

**The inner arc** (red) represents the goalkeeper's "diving envelope." Any shots placed in this area are within their reach and will be saved if they dive the right way.

The average speed of a penalty is 70 mph (112 kmh).

## SENSATIONAL SHOOT-OUT

The 1994 FIFA World Cup final was the first to be decided by a penalty shoot-out. Brazil won the game after Italy's star player, Roberto Baggio, ballooned the decisive penalty over the bar.

**The goalkeeper** can move, but must stay on or behind the goal line until the ball has been kicked.

**The orange arc** represents a zone in which the goalkeeper can still reach the ball by diving. Any shots placed here can still be saved.

**Penalties placed in the top corners** are unsavable, even by world-class goalkeepers. However, they carry a higher risk of missing the target.

That gives a goalkeeper **only 700 milliseconds** to save it.

A penalty shoot-out in the **2005 Namibian Cup** finished **17–16.**

**Deciding where to place the ball** when taking a penalty depends on a number of factors. Are you right- or left-footed? Is the goalkeeper right- or left-handed? How much of a risk are you prepared to take?

# Taking penalties

**The penalty kick** is one of the most dramatic moments in a football match. A **single kick** from the **penalty spot** can determine which team **wins or loses** a match, or even an entire tournament.

# Corners

A team wins a **corner** whenever the ball **crosses the byline** after touching an opposition player. A corner presents a chance to play the ball into a **good attacking** position.

**From a corner, the ball** can be played anywhere on the field, but the corner taker typically chooses either the far post, the near post, the penalty spot, or to the closest teammate. The aim is to create the best opportunity to score.

**The corner taker** is the team's dead-ball specialist, who is skilled at delivering the ball with great accuracy.

Far post corner

Near post corner

Penalty spot corner

**The ball must be** placed so it touches some part of the arc line that marks the corner.

## FAST FACTS

**From the 13,000 corners** taken in the English Premier League over two seasons (2011–13), 2,150 led to a shot attempt, of which only 370 resulted in a goal—equating to about three percent.

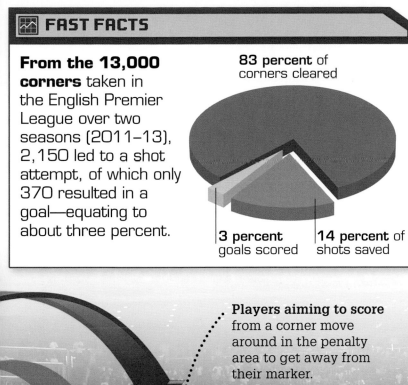

**83 percent** of corners cleared

**3 percent** goals scored

**14 percent** of shots saved

## TYPES OF CORNER

**Far post corner**
The ball is played into the area around the goalpost that is furthest away from the corner taker.

**Near post corner**
The ball is kicked to a tall teammate positioned at the goal closest to the corner arc, who uses the head to flick the ball across goal into a striker's path.

**Penalty spot corner**
The ball is delivered to an unmarked attacker in the penalty area who is in a position to shoot.

**Short corner**
The ball is passed to the nearest teammate who is in a better position to cross the ball into the penalty area.

**Players aiming to score** from a corner move around in the penalty area to get away from their marker.

One goal was scored from **every 29 corners** taken at the **2018 FIFA World Cup.**

Short corner

# The card system

If a player commits a **serious foul**, the referee shows the **offender** a card. A **yellow card** serves as a warning, whereas a **red card** means the player must leave the pitch right away.

English referee **Ken Aston** invented the **card system** after the 1966 FIFA World Cup.

**The referee points** to the dressing room immediately after showing the offender a red card. According to the laws, the sent-off player cannot remain on—or anywhere around—the field of play.

**The red and yellow cards** are sometimes kept in different pockets, so the referee avoids pulling out the wrong card in the heat of the moment.

## REFEREE'S NOTEBOOK

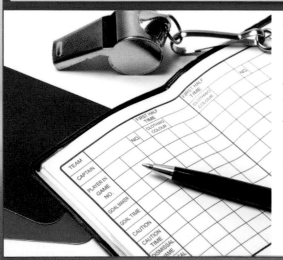

The referee uses a notebook to record key facts and incidents that occur in the game. This includes goal times, details of any substitutions made, and the names of players who have received a red or yellow card.

**The sent-off player** cannot be replaced. The team must play the rest of the game with one fewer player.

## FAST FACTS

**A player receives** a yellow card for offenses, such as those listed opposite. A red card is shown for very serious offenses, such as those listed below.

### Yellow card offenses

- Rough tackling
- Arguing with the referee
- Holding an opponent
- Blocking the goalkeeper
- Deliberate time wasting
- Refusing to move the correct distance from a free kick
- Deliberate handball
- Unsporting behavior

# Goal-line technology

Goal-line technology (GLT) is a **computerized system** introduced in 2012 to help officials in situations when it is difficult to tell whether or not the **ball has crossed the goal line** for a goal.

**HOW IT WORKS**:

**1** Seven fast frame cameras located above and around each goal track the ball's movement in the goal area.

**2** The cameras send the information to a computer that analyzes if the ball has crossed the goal line.

GoalControl

**Goal-line technology** is able to relay the result to the referee within a second of the incident taking place, which means there is no delay to the game.

## COSTLY ERRORS

Following several refereeing errors at the 2010 FIFA World Cup—including a disallowed England goal in their 4–1 defeat to Germany (above)—FIFA decided to bring in goal-line technology.

The GLT system only relays information to the game officials.

## FAST FACTS

**A goal is awarded** when the officials are sure that every part of the ball has crossed the goal line. Goal-line technology is highly accurate, with a margin of error of only 0.12 in (3 mm).

Goal line

Field

**Goal**

Goal line

Field

**No Goal**

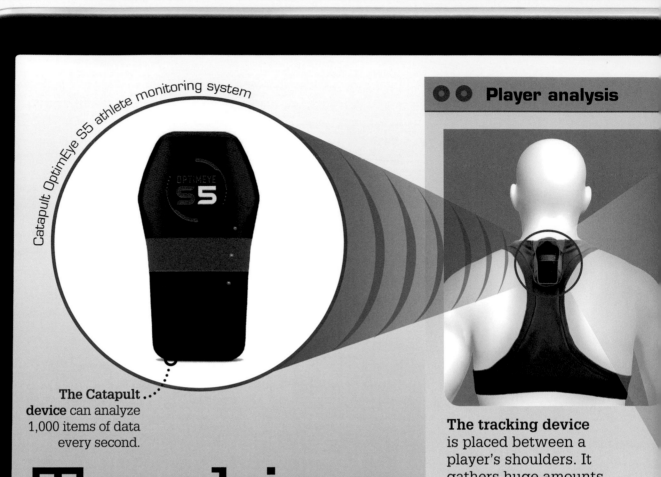

Catapult OptimEye S5 athlete monitoring system

**The Catapult device** can analyze 1,000 items of data every second.

# Tracking players

Many players wear a **tracking device** under their shirt. This provides **crucial information** about the player's **physical performance**.

## Player analysis

**The tracking device** is placed between a player's shoulders. It gathers huge amounts of information, which can be analyzed both during and after the game.

### PRECISION PASSING

Every pass a player makes in a game is also recorded. Blue arrows are successful passes; red arrows are unsuccessful ones.

**Data received**

### Heart rate
A program analyzes a player's heart rate during a game. Using this data, analysts can tell when players start to tire.

### Number of sprints
The number of sprints a player makes in a game is tracked. A drop in number may indicate player fatigue or injury.

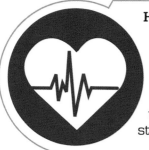

### Yards per minute
Logging the amount of ground a player covers every minute reveals a player's overall fitness or stamina.

### Total distance covered
The device also tracks the total amount of ground a player covers during the course of a game.

### High-speed running
Analysts can tell the total distance a player has sprinted in a game. The higher the number, the fitter the player.

### Acceleration
The device measures the total number of accelerations a player makes in a game, how long they last, and how much ground is covered.

### Dynamic stress load
By tracking a player's movement the device calculates how hard the player is working throughout the match.

### Deceleration
The total number of times a player slows down in a game is logged, and how much ground is covered.

# Over-time

## Gerardo Bedoya

has received **more red cards** than any other player in professional soccer. Capped **49 times** for Colombia, the defensive midfielder picked up **46 red cards** in a **20-year career** between 1995 and 2015.

BEDOYA

**Red cards** only became **compulsory** in **every** soccer game in **1982.**

The record for the *fastest dismissal* in a professional game is held by Bologna's **Giuseppe Lorenzo**. He was sent off after 10 seconds in an Italian Serie A game against Parma in 1990 for hitting an opponent.

00:10

## Team shirt sales

Bayern Munich sell more replica shirts per year than any other club in world soccer.

**1**
Bayern Munich
3,250,000

**2**
**Real Madrid**
3,050,000

**4**
Manchester United

**5**
Juventus
1,420,000

**Colombia's** Marcos Coll **is the only player** to score **directly from a corner** in a *FIFA World Cup final game*. He scored the wonder goal against the *Soviet Union*, at the **1962 tournament** in Chile.

# The longest

penalty shoot-out of all time in professional soccer occurred in a game between KK Palace and Civics in the Namibian Cup final in 2005. Forty-eight spot kicks were taken before KK Palace finally triumphed 17–16.

On **wet,** *rainy days,* leather soccer balls **could often double** in weight. **By the** *end of a game* **the ball could weigh as much as** **2.2 lb (1 kg).**

# Shirt sponsorship

Shirt sponsorship has become a major source of revenue for clubs around the world, but the amount of money raised in this way varies from league to league. England's Premier League leads the way.

$445.9 million

Premier League
**England**

$224.8 million

Bundesliga
**Germany**

$104.7 million

La Liga
**Spain**

$99.2 million

Serie A
**Italy**

$89.4 million

Ligue 1
**France**

# Individual Skills

Soccer is a fast-paced game in which players must have the skills to control the ball's movement. These skills include passing, shooting, tackling, volleying, heading, and dribbling. To be able to use these skills automatically in games, players practice them regularly in training.

# Ball control

Any player who receives the ball must be able to bring it **under control** right away. The **quicker** the player can do this, the more **time** and **space** there will be to decide the next move.

**1. Chest trap**
Lean back and cushion the ball with the chest. The key is to slow the ball's speed at the point of contact.

**2. Balance**
Use the arms for balance and also to shield the ball from any opponents.

**3. Ball position**
As the ball drops to the ground in front of you, get ready to make a pass or run with the ball.

The quality of the "first touch" determines how quickly a player can control the ball. The best players can put the ball exactly where they want it with a single touch.

Professional players use an average of two touches per possession.

## SKILL DRILL

**In tight situations,** use the top of the foot to control a ball that arrives at shin height, so you can make a pass or start a dribble.

Closely watch the ball as it comes to your foot.

Relax the foot as the ball lands on it.

# Passing

Passing is the most **efficient way** of **moving the ball** toward the opponent's goal. Skilled players are able to make passes accurately along the **ground**, in the **air**, and over a **range** of distances.

**The short pass** is the most accurate form of passing, in which the passer plays the ball to a teammate who is nearby.

**The passing player** strikes the ball with the side of his foot to make a short pass, the laces of the cleat for a long pass, and the outside of the foot for a wide, diagonal pass.

## SKILL DRILL

**A short pass** is a controlled pass made with the side of the foot. In this form of passing, the ball is kicked to a teammate along the ground and moves at a relatively slow speed.

**1.** Point the standing foot in the direction you want the ball to travel and strike the ball with the side of the foot.

Keep ankle locked at the point of contact.

**2.** Judge the length of the follow-through to ensure that the ball has enough pace to reach the intended target.

Sweep the striking foot across.

**The player making the pass** must be able to control the ball's speed and direction so that it reaches the intended teammate without being blocked by an opponent.

**The long ball** is played over a large distance toward the opponent's goal, in the hope that a teammate receives the ball and starts an attack.

**The wide, diagonal pass** is a long-range pass, normally made from inside the player's own half to a teammate near the touchline.

A long ball describes any pass that is longer than 35 yd (32 m).

## TIKI-TAKA

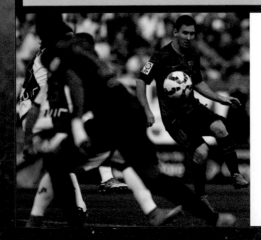

Tiki-taka is a style of play in which a team passes and moves at high speed, denying the opposition possession of the ball. The style was introduced in the mid-2000s by Spanish club Barcelona, who won the Champions League trophy three times between 2008 and 2015.

# Dribbling

The ability to move the ball past opposing players in tight spaces is known as **dribbling**. Good dribblers have **quick feet**, **great balance**, and create more goal-scoring chances.

**The best dribblers** keep the ball close to their feet. They move the ball using the inside and outside of both feet, as they twist and turn their way past defenders.

A player **dribbles** the ball an average distance of **208 yards (191 m)** in a game.

## DRIBBLING DYNAMO

During the 1986 FIFA World Cup quarter-final game against England, Argentina's star player Diego Maradona dribbled past five English players to score one of the most impressive goals in World Cup history.

**1. Look ahead**
Assess the situation in front as you move forward with the ball.

**2. Shoulder feint**
Drop the shoulder as though you are about to move in one direction, but take the ball the opposite way.

## SKILL DRILL

**The step over** is a trick used to fool an opponent into thinking you're about to make a pass when the real aim is to dribble past them.

Drop shoulder

**1.** Approach the ball as if you are about to pass it with the outside of the foot.

Place weight on the non-kicking foot

Look straight ahead

Swivel the foot around the ball

**2.** Instead of passing, move the foot around the ball and then dribble in the opposite direction.

**3. Beat the opponent**
Use the outside of your foot to move the ball away from the challenger. Keep the ball close to your feet.

# Shooting

If you want to be the team's **star goal scorer**, you will need **accurate shooting** skills. There are many shot types, but the most spectacular is the **power shot**, where a player **strikes the ball hard**, and hopes the **ball's speed** and direction will take it past the goalkeeper.

**1. Ball-watching**
Keep your eyes focused on the part of the ball you want to strike.

**2. Body position**
Keep your upper body over the ball during the shot so the ball stays low.

Fewer than three out of every 20 goal-scoring attempts result in a goal.

**When taking a power shot,** aim to kick the ball either side of the goalkeeper. The hardest places for the keeper to reach are the four corners of the net.

**5. Impact**
Make firm contact with the bottom right part of the ball and follow through with the kicking leg.

**3. Standing leg**
Line up the non-kicking foot alongside the ball with the toe pointing in the direction you want to aim the shot.

**4. Striking leg**
Sweep the shooting leg smoothly and strike the ball with the instep for an inswinging shot.

**GOAL MACHINE**

Brazilian legend Pele was among the finest goal scorers ever. In a glittering career that spanned 22 years (1955–77), he played 1,363 games and scored an amazing 1,281 goals.

# Volleying

**Striking the ball** while it is in midair is known as volleying. Watching a player volley the ball into the **back of the net** is one of the most **stunning sights** in soccer.

**3. Impact**
Strike the ball firmly with the top of the cleat.

**4. Leg position**
Keep the striking leg parallel to the ground during the follow through.

## LONGEST VOLLEY

During a German league game in 2014, SC Paderborn's player Moritz Stoppelkamp volleyed the ball 90 yards (82 meters) into an empty net to score the longest volleyed goal ever.

**1. Head and body**
Keep your head still and watch the ball closely throughout.

The **scissor kick** is a way of volleying a ball at waist height. Watch the ball's flight so you can time your leap correctly. While airborne, keep your legs apart like open scissors, then snap the kicking leg forward and strike the ball with power.

**SKILL DRILL**

The **bicycle kick** is an overhead volley where you kick the ball in the opposite direction to that in which you are facing.

Leap

**1.** Raise the non-kicking foot and leap into the air using the other foot.

Sweep

**2.** Once airborne, sweep the striking leg toward the ball.

Strike

**3.** Kick the ball over your head, and as you land, use the hand to cushion the impact.

**2. Hip movement**
Swivel the hips quickly toward the ball to generate maximum power.

Striking the ball on the **bounce** or a split-second after is known as a **half-volley.**

# Heading

Heading the ball is a vital skill for both **attackers** and **defenders**. Players who are expert headers **score more goals**, defend better, and win more battles for **possession**.

**Giant leap**
Time your leap correctly so that you meet the ball before any opposition players.

## A HEAD FOR GOAL

In the 2002 FIFA World Cup tournament, German forward Miroslav Klose scored five goals in total—all of them were headers.

**Firm contact**
Use the forehead. This provides the most accuracy and power.

**Pull up**
Use your arms to pull yourself as high into the air as possible.

## SKILL DRILL

**When making a** defensive header, the main aim is to knock the ball as far away as possible from the attacking player.

Use your forehead.

Leap up to meet the ball.

**For a power header**, the player leaps in the air and uses the neck muscles to sling his forehead to make contact with the ball.

Some players are able to leap up to 8 ft (2.4 m) to head the ball.

## 📊 FAST FACTS

**The chart opposite shows** the number of different types of challenge a defender typically makes to dispossess the opponent in a game.

| | |
|---|---|
| Tackle | ⚽⚽⚽ 3 |
| Header challenge | ⚽ 1 |
| Pressing opponent | ⚽ 1 |
| Blocking a shot or pass | ⚽⚽⚽⚽⚽⚽⚽⚽⚽⚽⚽⚽⚽⚽⚽⚽⚽⚽⚽ 19 |
| Clearing a long ball | ⚽ 1 |

**The slide tackle** is used by defenders as a last-ditch effort to dispossess an opponent, as the tackler ends up on the ground and out of the game. Unless the tackle is accurate, there is also a high chance of fouling (and even injuring) the attacker.

**1. Leg position**
Slide in with the tackling leg and knock the ball away from the attacker.

## SKILL DRILL

**The block tackle** is the safest type of tackle. To make this tackle, meet the attacker head on and block the ball as soon as the attacker tries to shoot or make a pass.

**1.** Stand in front of your opponent to deny them room.

**2.** Block the kick and make sure you keep the ankle firm.

# Tackling

A tackle is made to dispossess an **opponent**. The player must know how and when to make the tackle, so the ball is **won cleanly** without **fouling** or **injuring** the opponent.

The world's top defenders make about **5 tackles** in a game.

**3. Perfect timing**
Watch the ball closely to make sure you take it cleanly from the opponent.

**2. Support**
Use the arms to support the body on the ground.

# Over-time

Belgian goalkeeper **Kristof Van Hout** is officially the world's tallest-ever player, measuring **6 ft 10 in** *(2.08 m)*. Brazilian midfielder **Elton Gomes** is the **shortest,** standing at **5 ft 1 in** *(154 cm)*.

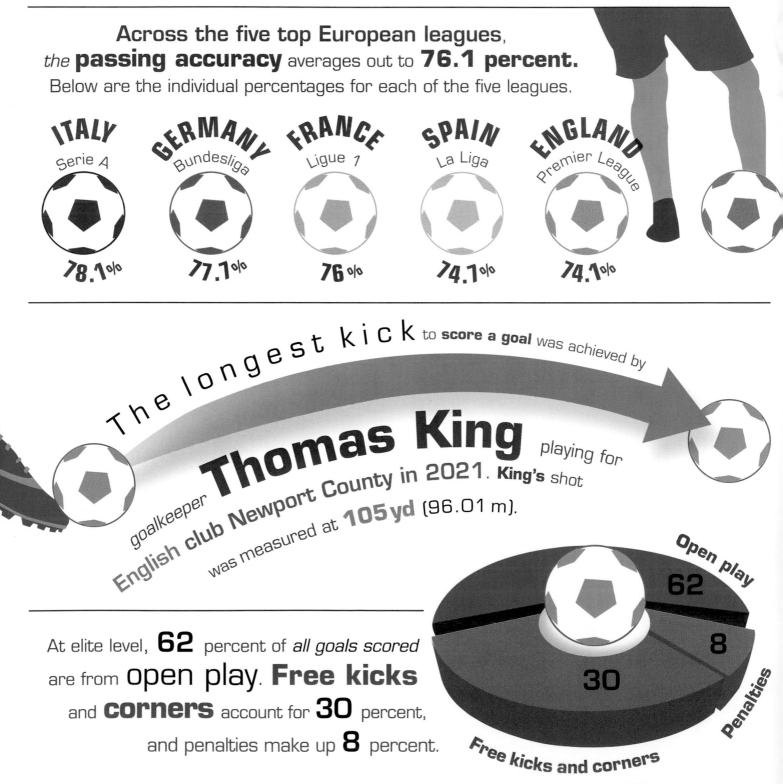

Across the five top European leagues, *the* **passing accuracy** averages out to **76.1 percent.** Below are the individual percentages for each of the five leagues.

**ITALY** Serie A — **78.1%**

**GERMANY** Bundesliga — **77.7%**

**FRANCE** Ligue 1 — **76%**

**SPAIN** La Liga — **74.7%**

**ENGLAND** Premier League — **74.1%**

The longest kick to **score a goal** was achieved by **Thomas King** playing for goalkeeper English **club** Newport County in 2021. **King's** shot was measured at **105 yd** (96.01 m).

At elite level, **62** percent of *all goals scored* are from **open play. Free kicks** and **corners** account for **30** percent, and penalties make up **8** percent.

Open play **62**

Penalties **8**

**30** Free kicks and corners

**A goal in every minute!**

Cristiano Ronaldo, Luis Suarez, and **Zlatan Ibrahimovic** have all scored **in each minute**, from the **1st** to the **90th**, in competitive football.

The world record for the **longest headed goal** is *63.4yd (58m)* scored by Odd's BK's **Joan Samuelsen** in 2011 against Tromso in the **Norwegian Eliteserien** league.

The **best way** to spend the 15-minute halftime break is to *rest* for the first **7.5 minutes** and then use the **other half** to do *light activity* to warm up the **muscles**.

**Bayern Munich's**

# Alphonso Davies

is the world's fastest player. He has been clocked sprinting at **22.7 mph (36.51 kph)**, and is nicknamed **"Roadrunner"** by his teammates.

The most goals scored by a **single player** in a FIFA *World Cup finals tournament* was **13** by **Just Fontaine** of France in 1958.

# A team game

Soccer is a team game of
11 players, who must work
together to beat the opposition.
The manager helps them
achieve this by making sure
they practice effectively on the
training field, by picking a
formation to suit the players'
strengths, and by making
sure that the 11 players
know their roles.

# Goalkeeping

The goalkeeper is allowed to **handle** the ball inside the team's **penalty area**, but nowhere else on the field. As the team's last line of defense, this key player has to be **quick** and good at **leaping**, **catching**, and **kicking**.

**HIGH ACHIEVER**

Spanish goalkeeper Iker Casillas won many trophies with his club team Real Madrid between the years 1999 and 2015. This includes five league titles, four Spanish Super Cups, three Champions League trophies, the Copa Del Rey twice, and the UEFA Super Cup twice.

**Pay close attention** to the game, anticipate any dangers, and be ready to stop any shots.

**Stay on your toes** at all times, so you can leap in either direction to make a save.

**The goalkeeper** must always be ready to make a diving save, as skillful attackers tend to direct their shots into the corners of the goal.

**Reach the ball** with an outstretched hand and push it out of play.

**Keep the wrist locked** to keep the ball from slipping through the hands.

Christiane Engler, keeper for French club PSG, conceded only 4 goals in the 2020-21 season.

## MARSHALING THE DEFENSE

The goalkeeper is not just a shot-stopper, but also the leader in defense. It is the goalkeeper's job to organize the defenders so they can deal with any threats to goal. When defending free kicks, the goalkeeper forms the defensive wall by telling the defenders where to stand.

### Fullback
Fullbacks operate on either side of the field and defend the touchline. When one fullback goes on a forward run, the other will move across to support the center backs.

### Wingback
Two wingbacks operate on either side of the field, but slightly up the field compared to the fullback. Wingbacks are responsible for both attacking and defending along the touchline.

**GAME STATS**
**Distance:** 6.2 miles (10.0 km)
**Tackles:** 2.0
**Passes:** 41.2
**Clearances:** 3.2

**GAME STATS**
**Distance:** 5.9 miles (9.5 km)
**Tackles:** 1.7
**Passes:** 41.9
**Clearances:** 5.9

**The sweeper** was an important position in the past, but is rarely seen in the modern game. Not a single team used one at the 2014 FIFA World Cup.

### Center back
A team places two center backs in front of the goalkeeper. They mark the opposition's most advanced forwards, and their main role is to clear the ball from the penalty area.

### Sweeper
The sweeper plays behind the center-backs and has no specific marking duties. In the modern game, the goalkeeper often takes on part of the traditional role of the sweeper.

Dutch center back Ronald Koeman scored **253 goals** in his career— **a record for a defender**.

## THE GREAT DEFENDER

A FIFA World Cup winner with West Germany in 1974, Franz Beckenbauer is considered one of the greatest defenders in soccer history. He redefined the role of a sweeper, from simply being a defensive stopper to becoming a team's creative attacking force.

**GAME STATS**
Distance: 6.6 miles (10.6 km)
Tackles: 1.5
Passes: 34.8
Dribbles: 2.1

ATTACK

ATTACK

ATTACK

ATTACK

# Solid defending

A defender's main job is **to stop the opponent from scoring a goal**. There are **four types** of defender: fullback, wingback, center back, and sweeper (also known as a "libero").

**Defenders must operate as a unit**, but each has a different role to play. Fullbacks make the most tackles, center backs execute the most clearances, while wingbacks have to run the farthest.

**Defensive midfielder**
This player's role is to stop an opponent's attack, and to cover in defense if one of his team's defenders joins an attack. Defensive midfielders will rarely advance into an opponent's half.

**Central midfielder**
In attack, central midfielders pass the ball and look to join the forward. In defense, they drop back to help the defenders stop an opponent's attack.

**GAME STATS**
**Distance:** 5.5 miles (8.9 km)
**Tackles:** 5.5
**Passes:** 48.6
**Dribbles:** 0.9

Manchester City's **Ilkay Gündogan** made a world record **174 passes** against Chelsea in 2017–18.

**GAME STATS**
**Distance:** 6.4 miles (10.3 km)
**Tackles:** 2.4
**Passes:** 47.3
**Dribbles:** 1.2

**GAME STATS**
**Distance:** 5.7 miles (9.1 km)
**Tackles:** 2.1
**Passes:** 43.0
**Dribbles:** 1.6

# Midfield magic

Midfielders **break up** an opponent's play and **set in motion** their own team's attack. There are **four types of midfielder**: defensive midfielder, central midfielder, wide midfielder, and attacking midfielder.

**Wide midfielder**
A wide midfielder is positioned closer to the touchline. In attack, their main role is to provide crosses into the opponent's penalty area. In defense, they must drop back to provide extra cover.

**Attacking midfielder**
The attacking midfielder is the creative force of a team and a link between the midfield and a striker. Attacking midfielders only have a limited defensive role and rarely drop back in their own half.

**Midfielders have a crucial role to play** in both defense and attack, with each type of player having to perform different tasks. Defensive midfielders average the most tackles per game, while central midfielders run the farthest. The number of midfield players a team fields depends on its formation.

DEFENSE

ATTACK

ATTACK

ATTACK

ATTACK

**GAME STATS**
Distance: 6.3 miles (10.1 km)
Tackles: 1.7
Passes: 39.5
Dribbles: 1.3

**MIDFIELD MASTER**

Johan Cruyff was the best midfielder of his generation. During his 20-year career, he won eight Dutch league titles, one Spanish league title, and led the Netherlands to the FIFA World Cup final in 1974.

# Flying forwards

**Forwards** are the players who are positioned **closest to an opponent's goal**. Their main job is to **score goals**, and they are often a team's most-celebrated, and expensive, players.

DEFENSE

DEFENSE

ATTACK

Forwards have to be **fast**. Some can run as fast as **10.6 yd (9.7 m) per second**.

**GAME STATS**
**Distance:** 5.8 miles (9.4 km)
**Tackles:** 0.9
**Passes:** 28.5
**Shots:** 1.5

**No.10/Second striker**
The No.10 (also known as the second striker), plays in the space between an opponent's defense and midfield, commonly known as "the hole." From there, they will set up attacks or shoot for goal.

**Winger**
Part of an attacking formation, a winger is responsible for attacking down the edges of the field and for sending crosses into the penalty box. Wingers have limited defensive duties.

**Center forward**
A center forward's main job is to score goals and so they spend most of their time operating in an area in front of the opponent's goal. From here, they are in the best position to receive balls, turn, and score.

## TOP STRIKE PARTNERSHIP

Two of the greatest forwards the game has ever seen, Alfredo Di Stéfano (left) and Ferenc Puskás combined with devastating effect for Real Madrid. Together, they propelled the Spanish giants to four consecutive league titles (1961–64) and two European Cups (1959 and 1960), and scored a staggering 258 goals in 182 league games.

**GAME STATS**
**Distance:** 5.5 miles (8.9 km)
**Tackles:** 0.4
**Passes:** 18.3
**Shots:** 2.1

**GAME STATS**
**Distance:** 5.8 miles (9.3 km)
**Tackles:** 1.0
**Passes:** 25.7
**Shots:** 1.7

ATTACK

DEFENSE

**Forwards have many different roles.** Center forwards average the most shots per game. No.10s and wingers have to create goal-scoring opportunities for the center forward.

# Formations

A formation is the **way a team lines up on the field**. It is normally **described using a string of numbers**, which represent the number of players in each area of the field.

AC Milan won the Champions League in 1989 and 1990 using a **4-4-2**.

## 4-4-2

**The classic 4-4-2 formation** has two lines of four in defense and midfield, with two forwards.

**Two wide midfielders** provide crosses for the two forwards in attack. They must also drop back to help out in defense.

**Fullbacks** have a vital role to play in defense, but will often be used as extra attackers.

**Forwards** can advance to the opponent's goal without having to wait for support from the midfield.

### ✔ Advantages

- Two lines of four provide greater defensive cover.
- A pair of strikers creates a constant attacking threat.
- Fullbacks provide extra width to stretch an opponent's defense.

### ✘ Disadvantages

- With only two central midfielders, a team can easily be outnumbered in midfield.
- Opponent can exploit the space between defense and midfield—called "the hole."
- This system places great pressure on midfielders both to attack and defend.

# 4-2-3-1

The dominant formation at the turn of the 21st century, this is still the preferred system in much of Europe.

**Four defenders** create a solid line of defense. The fullbacks are expected to advance to create width in attack.

**Wide midfielders** have a vital role to play both in attack and defense.

**Defensive midfielders** provide extra cover in defense.

**The single striker** relies on support from the three attacking midfielders.

## ✔ Advantages

- It is easy to pass the ball through midfield.
- This system makes it hard for teams to be overrun in midfield.
- Three attacking midfielders provide a greater number of attacking options.

## ✘ Disadvantages

- The single striker relies on support from attacking midfielders.
- Attacking midfielders have to work very hard to cover in both defense and attack.
- This system places great responsibility on the wide players to drop back to help out in defense.

# Other modern formations

**4-1-2-1-2**
Also known as "The Diamond," this formation provides greater solidity in midfield. Fullbacks can move forward to provide the width in attack.

**4-3-3**
Three midfielders move across the field as a unit. Because it has more attackers, many teams adopt this system if they are chasing a game.

**4-3-2-1**
Named the "Christmas Tree" after its pointed shape, this is a more attacking variation of the 4-3-3, with two players playing behind a single striker.

# More formations

## 4-5-1

A packed midfield means this is the formation of choice for teams looking to avoid defeat in knockout competitions.

**Two wide midfielders** can push forward in attack to make a 4-3-3.

**Defenders** can sit deeper, due to the packed midfield.

A single striker has to keep possession of the ball in attack and wait for support.

### ✔ Advantages
- A five-player midfield normally leads to more possession of the ball.
- The formation is flexible. For example, it is easy to switch to a 4-3-3 in attack.
- This is a difficult formation for an opponent to break down.

### ✘ Disadvantages
- It is easy for the single striker to become isolated.
- The formation makes it difficult for teams to execute counterattacks.
- Great pressure is placed on central midfielders to join the striker in attack.

## BRAZIL BREAKS THE MOLD

Developed to strengthen the defense without losing any numbers in attack, the 4-2-4 formation burst onto the scene when Brazil won the 1958 FIFA World Cup. In practice, it operates as a 4-3-3 in defense and as a 3-3-4 in attack.

Many think a 4-6-0 formation, with no striker, will be the formation of the future.

# 5-3-2/3-5-2

A pair of wingbacks provides extra options in both defense and attack, but they have to be incredibly fit to make the formation work.

**The middle defender** in the three-player defense must be good at passing, and is usually responsible for launching attacks.

**Wingbacks** provide width in attack and extra cover in defense.

**Midfielders** provide cover in defense and extra options in attack.

**A pair of strikers** can move forward to attack without having to wait for extra support from midfield.

## ✔ Advantages

- Three central defenders reduce the threat of an opponent's counterattack.
- The defensive unit is usually helped by a deep-lying midfielder.
- Three midfielders and wingbacks provide a variety of attacking options.

## ✘ Disadvantages

- The back three must include at least one player who is good at passing the ball.
- Players require a superb sense of positioning to play in this formation.

# Old formations

**2-3-5**
Known as "The Pyramid," this was the standard formation of the 1880s. It placed a huge emphasis on attacking.

**3-2-2-3 (also known as WM)**
First used in the 1920s, this formation reinforced the defense to counter the increased attacking threat that came about from a change in the offside rule.

Sweeper

**1-4-3-2**
Known as "catenaccio," this formation saw a sweeper (or "libero") positioned between the goalkeeper and the defense to add more defensive steel.

# Set pieces: attacking

**Corners** and **free kicks** are called **set pieces**. They provide teams with the perfect opportunity to **execute set moves** they have spent **hours rehearsing** on the training ground.

**The attacking side** will often position a player in front of the near post. This player will look to flick the ball on with his head.

**Where the corner taker** delivers the ball will depend on the set move planned.

**The players who are the best headers** in the attacking team will line up near the edge of the penalty area and run toward goal as the corner is taken.

## 📊 FAST FACTS

**Although corners** represent a good goal-scoring opportunity, not as many goals are scored from them as you might think.

**5**

Average number of corners a team wins in a game.

**75**

One in 75 corners taken leads directly to a goal.

**45**

One in 45 corners taken leads indirectly to a goal.

**18**

Percentage of goals scored from corners at the 2018 FIFA World Cup.

**At least one player is left** near the edge of the penalty area to pounce on any rebounds. They could also be a set move option for the corner taker.

# Set piece: free kick

**If a free kick is awarded** too far away for a direct shot on goal, the attacking side will look to use a set move they have practiced on the training ground.

**Option 1: Clipped cross**
The free kick taker will look to swing the ball toward the edge of the six-yard box. Attackers will run toward the goal to meet the incoming ball.

**Option 2: Short pass**
The free kick taker plays a short pass to a teammate, who runs to the byline before crossing the ball.

**The defending team** will normally form a high defensive line to try to catch an attacking player offside.

**①**

**②**

**One attacking player** will look to block the goalkeeper.

**The defenders** in this scenario are using the zonal defense system.

## Set piece: corner
The attacking team will set up in the same way for most corners. Where the ball is delivered will depend on the set move the attacking side has chosen to execute.

At the 2018 FIFA World Cup, 2 in every 5 goals scored came from a set-piece.

**Another attacking player** will make a run toward the far post, in case the corner taker delivers a long corner.

# Set pieces: defending

Because **set pieces** offer such a good goal-scoring opportunity, it is **vital that a defense is organized** to deal with the impending threat.

**Teams use two main systems** when they are defending corners: zonal marking or man marking.

**The corner taker** delivers the ball into the penalty area.

## Zonal marking

Defenders take up set positions at corner kicks, and defend a particular area, or zone, rather than marking an opposing player.

**Defenders move toward the ball** as the corner is taken.

**At least one defender** stays on the edge of the penalty area to launch an attack.

**One player stands on each post.** This makes it harder for an opponent to score a goal.

**Each yellow square** represents a zone for which a single defender is responsible.

### ✔ Advantages
- Leaves the goalkeeper free to come and collect the ball, because the area around them is likely to be less congested.
- Defending becomes a team responsibility.

### ✗ Disadvantages
- It is easier for attackers to win a header, because, as they have a further distance to run toward the ball, they can arrive at it at greater speed and leap higher.

# Defensive walls for free kicks

The goalkeeper decides how many players should be in a defensive wall. That number depends on where the free kick is taken from. Each segment in this illustration shows how many players would be in a wall if a free kick is taken inside it.

# One-on-one-marking

Each defender picks up an opposition player, and is responsible for staying with them until the ball has been cleared and the danger is over.

**The corner taker** delivers the ball into the penalty area.

**Attackers** will try to lose their marker to get a free run at the ball.

**One defender stands on each post**, as with zonal marking.

**Defenders must always stay goalside** of the attacker they are marking.

## ✔ Advantages

- Defenders can get the same run at the ball as attackers.

## ✗ Disadvantages

- Defenders can get dragged around the penalty area by attackers.
- The system places great responsibility on the individual defender not to lose the attacker they are marking.
- The area around the goal mouth can become congested, making it difficult for the goalkeeper to come and claim the ball.

# Soccer genius

Every team takes to the field with a **strategy** to help them win the game. This is devised by the **manager**, based on a **style of play** the team has developed over many years.

**1930s**

**1870s**

**The passing method** of play was introduced in 1870 by Scottish side Queen of the South. The team revolutionized the game from one that was solely based on dribbling.

**Herbert Chapman** founded the WM formation in the 1930s while managing English club Arsenal. The strategy focused on defense—previously the game was all about attacking.

**Helenio Herrera** managed Italian side Inter Milan to European Cup glory in 1964 and 1965. Using a defensive style called catenaccio, the team won games by scoring on the counterattack.

**1960s**

Hungary scored a record 27 goals at the 1954 FIFA World Cup.

**The era of modern soccer** has seen the emergence of many different strategies and playing styles. Here is a selection that have led to great success on the field.

**Hungary** played a unique formation in the 1950s, which saw the striker swap roles with midfielders, pulling opposition players out of position. The team won the Olympic gold medal in 1952.

**1950s**

## 2000s

**The Netherlands team** of the 1970s adopted a style of play known as Total Football, in which players swapped roles on the field. The team was a FIFA World Cup finalist in 1974 and 1978.

**Pep Guardiola's** reign at Spanish club Barcelona saw the side using a possession-based style called Tiki-taka to win multiple trophies between 2008–2012.

## 1970s

**Vicente del Bosque** masterminded Spain's FIFA World Cup triumph in 2010. The team used a system called the False Nine, which features no recognized striker, but a trio of attacking midfielders instead.

## 2010

## 2010s

### RINUS MICHELS

Rinus Michels is credited as inventing Total Football. In 1971, he led Dutch side Ajax to the first of three successive European Cup wins. He also introduced the style of play to Spanish side Barcelona and the Netherlands team, (leading the Dutch to European Championship glory in 1988).

**Jürgen Klopp,** as manager of Borussia Dortmund then of Liverpool, has achieved huge success with his Gegenpressing strategy. In this style of play, his team moves farther up the pitch every time it loses possession, in order to win back the ball as quickly as possible.

# Overtime

The **average** number of **goals scored per game** across the top leagues in **China, England, France, Germany, Italy, Spain,** and the **US** is **2.68**.

German club **Bayern Munich** made a *record* **1,033 passes** in their **3–1** win over **Hertha Berlin** in a 2014 **Bundesliga match.**

During a **90-minute game** (excluding injury time), the **actual time the ball is in play** ranges between **60–65 minutes**. At non-professional level, the figure is between **50–55 minutes.**

The **most common scoreline** in soccer games is 1–1, making up **11** percent of all results. Here are the percentages of other common scorelines.

- **2–3** 2%
- **4–1** 2%
- **4–0** 2%
- **0–3** 2%
- **3–2** 2%
- **1–3** 3%
- **0–2** 4%
- **3–1** 4%
- **3–0** 4%
- **2–2** 5%
- **1–2** 6%
- **0–1** 7%
- **2–0** 8%
- **0–0** 8%
- **2–1** 8%
- **1–0** 10%
- **1–1** 11%
- **All other scores** 12%

A study of the English Premier League reveals **when goals** are **commonly scored** during a game.

| | |
|---|---|
| 0–15 minutes | **12.6% of goals** |
| 16–30 minutes | **13.7% of goals** |
| 31–45 minutes | **18.0% of goals** |
| 46–60 minutes | **14.4% of goals** |
| 61–75 minutes | **18.5% of goals** |
| 76–90 minutes | **22.8% of goals** |

In professional soccer, the **team that scores first** has only a **one in seven chance** of losing the game.

## The longest-ever **undefeated run of matches** in Europe's top four leagues are:

**AC Milan**
(Italy)
*1991–93*

**58 MATCHES**

**Bayern Munich**
(Germany)
*2012–14*

**53 MATCHES**

**Arsenal**
(England)
*2003–4*

**49 MATCHES**

**Juventus**
(Italy)
*2011–12*

**49 MATCHES**

**Liverpool**
(England)
*2019–20*

**44 MATCHES**

On average, **9** out of every **100 shots** result in a **goal**. In contrast, **12** out of every **100 headers** on goal end up in the *back of the net*.

Dutch side Ajax won all **46 home games** for *two seasons in a row* (**1971–72 and 1972–73**), also picking up **four titles**:

the **Dutch league title**, the KNVB Cup, the **European Cup**, and the Intercontinental Cup.

A soccer team is part of a much larger organization—the club, which has its own identity and tradition. Top clubs are run as businesses and employ hundreds of people. There are many different jobs to be done to keep a club running, from managing the team to selling tickets to fans and preparing the field for game day.

# Running a club

A large soccer club **employs people** with many different skills to ensure it **succeeds on the field** and as a **business.**

This diagram shows the different people who work at a soccer club, and explains what they do and how they work together to make sure that the club runs smoothly.

English club **Notts County** is recognized as **the world's first professional** soccer club.

The directors are often part owners of the club. They make the decisions about the club and its future plans.

**BOARD OF DIRECTORS**

The commercial director's role involves negotiating deals with sponsors and other businesses.

**COMMERCIAL DIRECTOR**

The chief executive officer (CEO) manages the day-to-day running of the whole club, and reports to the board of directors.

**CEO**

The manager is in charge of the first team. They control training, pick the team, and set the tactics for every game.

**FIRST TEAM MANAGER**

The financial director looks after the club's funds, and makes sure the club stays solvent.

**FINANCIAL DIRECTOR**

The technical director devises the coaching programs and is also in charge of signing of new players.

**TECHNICAL DIRECTOR**

CLUB DOCTOR

The doctor provides medical advice and care for the players.

PHYSICAL THERAPIST

The physical therapist takes care of injured players and helps the team stay injury-free.

FIRST TEAM

The team is picked from a total squad of 20–30 players.

ASSISTANT MANAGER

The assistant manager helps the first team manager prepare the team for every game.

COACHES

Coaches are responsible for the team's training. Each coach specializes in a different aspect of training.

SCOUTS

Scouts attend other soccer games on behalf of the club and look out for talented players.

YOUTH SOCCER DEVELOPMENT MANAGER

The youth soccer development manager is in charge of the local youth leagues.

LOCAL SOCCER DEVELOPMENT OFFICER

The development officer organizes and delivers a range of soccer activities for the local community.

HEAD OF SALES

The head of sales oversees the sale of tickets and club merchandise.

# The manager

Managers have to juggle **many tasks**. They are responsible for every aspect of **every team at a club**, from youth team to the first XI, and must also **speak to journalists**.

**A manager's main task** is to make sure the team wins as many games as possible. However, a manager's day does not end with the final whistle. They still have many other tasks to perform.

Guy Roux managed French club Auxerre for 44 years (1961–2005).

In the spotlight

- Dealing with the media.
- Preparing program notes.
- Helping club sponsors.
- Attending club events.
- Appearing on the club's media channels.

## Team and players

- Deciding on formations.
- Selecting the team.
- Motivating the players.
- Giving team talks before and during the match.
- Making substitutions during the match.

## Behind the scenes

- Maintaining player discipline.
- Running the club.
- Overseeing player development.
- Setting coaching policy.

## Running the club

- Buying and selling players.
- Appointing coaching staff.
- Overseeing coaching activities.
- Attending board meetings.
- Scouting for new players.

## MANAGERIAL MERRY-GO-ROUND

England
Italy
Spain
France
Germany

The job of a top-tier soccer manager is among the least secure in the world. This chart shows the average number of managerial changes each year in Europe's top-five leagues.

The Allianz Arena is lit in **different colors** when different teams play there.

## 🖼 KEY

1 Team bus parking bay
2 Players' entrance
3 Visiting team changing room
4 Home team changing room
5 Warm-up room
6 Game officials' room
7 Press conference hall

**Opened in 2005**, the Allianz Arena in Germany can hold up to 75,000 fans, making it among Europe's largest soccer venues. Bayern Munich play home matches there, and the German national team also regularly plays at the stadium.

### Players' entrance

A separate entrance allows players to enter the stadium privately, and avoid the large crowd of fans in the stadium.

# The stadium

A team's stadium features a field surrounded by **thousands of seats** for fans who come to watch the matches. It also includes all the **facilities** players need to prepare for a game.

### Locker room

The locker room is where players change into their uniforms and gather for the captain's final team talk.

### The tunnel

The players' tunnel leads on to the field. Players of both teams line up in the tunnel before the game.

A scout's job is to find talented new players. Larger clubs may have as many as 15 scouts.

Player scouted

# Transfers

Professional soccer has two **transfer windows**: the first runs from July to September, and the second is in January. They are an exciting time for soccer fans, but **how do transfers actually work?**

**Finding the right player** is only the start of a long process. A club has to go through many stages before a player officially signs for them.

The bid

Negotiations begin

**Once a club has found a player** it wants, it will make a bid to the club the player currently plays for. It may take several bids before one is accepted.

**After the bid has been accepted**, a club starts contract talks with a player's agent. The two parties must agree on details such as wages and performance-related bonuses.

## WORTH HIS WEIGHT IN GOLD

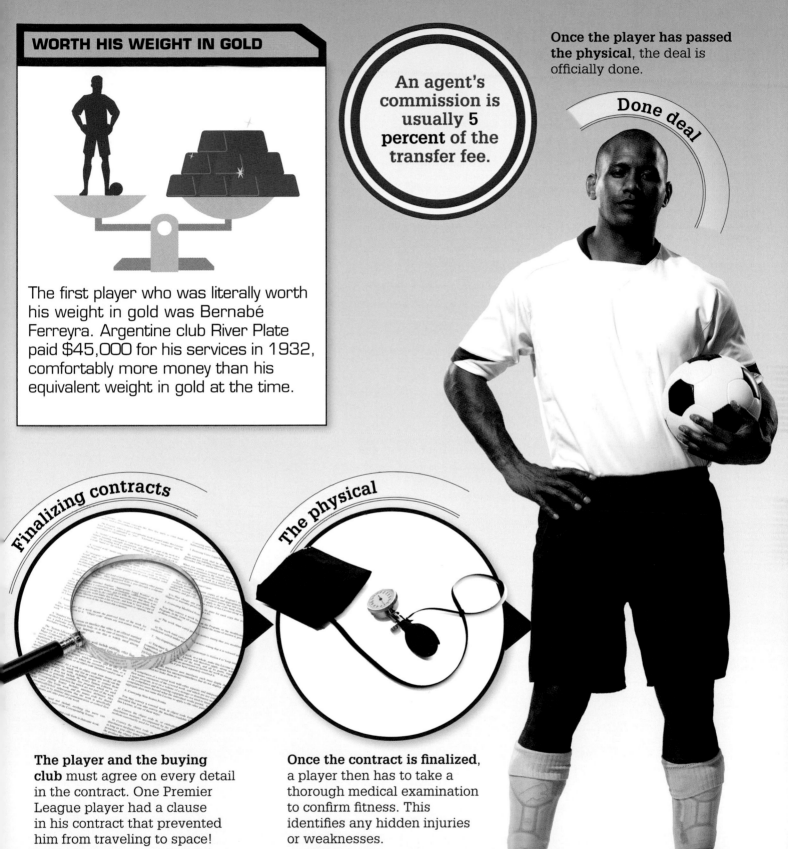

The first player who was literally worth his weight in gold was Bernabé Ferreyra. Argentine club River Plate paid $45,000 for his services in 1932, comfortably more money than his equivalent weight in gold at the time.

An agent's commission is usually **5 percent** of the transfer fee.

**Once the player has passed the physical**, the deal is officially done.

Done deal

Finalizing contracts

The physical

**The player and the buying club** must agree on every detail in the contract. One Premier League player had a clause in his contract that prevented him from traveling to space!

**Once the contract is finalized**, a player then has to take a thorough medical examination to confirm fitness. This identifies any hidden injuries or weaknesses.

# Training

Players mainly **practice** their **ball skills** during training, but also work on their **speed** and **agility**, **stamina**, **strength**, and **tactical awareness**.

*Speed and agility*

**High-intensity exercises**, such as sprints around obstacles, shuttle runs, hurdle hopping, and squat jumps, all help to improve a player's speed and agility.

📊 **FAST FACTS**

Soccer  7–9.5 miles (11–15 km)

Rugby  4–7 miles (6.5 –11 km)

Hockey  4–5 miles (6.5–8 km)

Tennis  3–5 miles (5–8 km)

Basketball  2–3 miles (3–5 km)

Football  1.25 miles (2 km)

Soccer players are exceptionally fit. They typically cover a distance of between 7–9.5 miles (11–15 km) during a 90-minute game.

*Ball skills*

**Players regularly train** their ball skills. The also play practice games in which they work on set pieces and different modes of attack and defense.

Professional players spend an **average** of three hours a day training.

## HYDRATION

During training, players shed between 2–3 lb (1–1.5 kg) of weight through sweat loss. The amount can rise to 6½ lb (3 kg) during a game played on a hot day. To stay hydrated, experts recommend that players consume about 40–50 fl oz (1.2–1.5 liters) of fluid for each 2 lb (1 kg) of weight they lose.

### Stamina

### Strength

### Tactical awareness

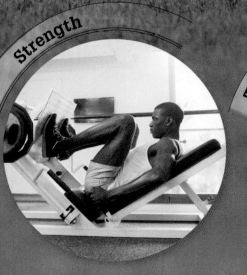

**The team performs stamina-building exercises** such as running and circuit drills. All players must be fit enough to play a full game without tiring.

**Gym workouts are specially** devised to develop players' leg muscles and overall body strength.

**The coach works with the players** to make sure they know their roles and can follow the game plan during the high-pressure situation of a game.

# Injury time

Soccer is a physical game in **which** players have to **sprint, jump, twist, turn,** and **tackle.** These actions place huge stress on the **muscles, joints,** and **bones,** and can sometimes cause **injuries.**

**The red circles highlight** the parts of the body that players are most likely to injure in a game. The number inside each circle refers to the number of injuries suffered in that area of the body out of every 100 injuries.

**Concussion**
Head injury resulting from a collision with another player.

**Shoulder dislocation**
Dislodged shoulder bone caused by an awkward fall.

Professional players sustain an average of **two injuries** per season.

**Back strain**
Muscle sprain or tear from overstretching the spine.

**Broken finger**
An injury suffered mostly by goalkeepers.

**Dead leg**
Severe bruising of the muscle resulting from a hard blow.

**Shin splints**
Tiny fractures caused by constant impact.

**Groin strain**
Overstretching of the groin muscle, caused by overreaching for the ball.

**Hamstring strain**
Muscle sprain caused by sprinting to chase the ball.

**Calf strain**
Muscle sprain or tear from overstretching the lower leg.

**Twisted ankle**
Severe sprain caused by turning too rapidly or a bad tackle.

**Thigh strain**
Tear or spraining of the thigh muscle, caused by overuse.

**Knee ligament damage**
Overbending of the knee joint, usually caused by a reckless tackle.

**Metatarsal fracture**
Cracked foot bone usually caused from a tackle with raised studs.

**Achilles strain**
Strained tendon in heel resulting from overuse.

# THE PHYSICAL THERAPIST'S ROLE

The physical therapist treats players who get injured during a game and helps with their recovery afterward. The physical therapist also assesses the fitness of players, and helps to devise individual training programs that ensure that the players stay fit throughout the season.

# A player's **week**

Most professional soccer players lead very **disciplined lives**. They follow a **strict routine** to ensure that they are **fully prepared** for a game. This includes getting as much **rest** as possible between games.

**ICE BATHS**

After a game, players take ice baths to treat muscle soreness. The cold makes blood vessels tighten, restricting blood flow to the muscles. When the player gets out of the bath, the blood vessels expand again and oxygen-rich blood floods into the muscles, speeding the recovery process.

|  | Monday | Tuesday |
|---|---|---|
| MORNING | Aerobic training | Practice game |
| AFTERNOON | Individual ball skills | Physical thera... session |
|  | Strength training | Medical assessment/ fitness test |
| EVENING | Free time | Free time |

**Below is an example** of a professional player's weekly schedule. It reveals just how much training is involved. Recovery time is equally important—players need about 8–10 hours of sleep a night.

Professional soccer players spend about **15 hours** a week training with the ball.

| Wednesday | Thursday | Friday | Saturday | Sunday |
|---|---|---|---|---|
| Tactical preparation | Recovery—light and low impact workout | Power and speed training session | Group ball skills | Recovery—light and low impact workout |
| Stretching—focus on flexibility | Post-game debrief led by the manager | Practice game | Travel to away game on team bus | Post-game debrief led by the manager |
| Group ball skills | Individual ball skills | Tactical preparation | AWAY GAME K.O.: 3:00pm | Physical therapy session |
| HOME GAME: K.O.: 7:45pm | Free time | Free time | Travel back from away game | Free time |

# The fans

True **soccer fans** are not just spectators, but eager participants who think of themselves as the team's **"twelfth" player**. They **chant**, **sing**, and voice their **opinions**, creating the **lively atmosphere** that spurs the team on.

**Replica jerseys, hats, and scarves** bearing the team's colors are worn to the game.

**Eight out of 10 fans** believe that their support helps the team to play better.

**Fans revel in the loud** and energetic atmosphere they create in the stadium. Some look forward to being around fellow fans as much as watching the game itself.

## FAST FACTS

**4 billion**

Soccer

**2.5 billion**

Cricket

**2.2 billion**

Basketball

**2 billion**

Tennis

**1 billion**

Volleyball

**0.9 billion**

Field hockey

**0.5 billion**

Baseball

**Soccer has a global fan base** of about 4 billion, which is more than any other sport in the world. About 64 percent of these fans are male and 36 percent are female.

**Some fans wave** flags to show their support.

**Die-hard fans often use the melody** of popular songs to make up catchy chants.

## FAN POWER

Across world soccer, statistics show that home sides win around half of their matches and lose just one in four. This might be down to the atmosphere home fans create, giving their side a mental edge against the visiting team.

# Overtime

## Europe's **longest-serving soccer managers** are:

| | |
|---|---|
| | **Ignacio Quereda:** 27 yr (1988–2015) at Spain (National women's team) |
| 5 | **Alex Ferguson:** 27 yr (1986–2013) at Manchester United (England) |
| 4 | **Ronnie McFall:** 30 yr (1986–2016) at Portadown (Northern Ireland) |
| 3 | **Bill Struth:** 34 yr (1920–1954) at Rangers (Scotland) |
| 2 | **Willie Maley:** 43 yr (1897–1940) at Celtic (Scotland) |
| 1 | **Guy Roux:** 44 yr (1961–2005) at Auxerre (France) |

## The football clubs with the **most followers** on **social media** are:

**1**
**Real Madrid**
*(Spain)*
**271 million** fans

**2**
**Barcelona**
*(Spain)*
**270 million** fans

**3**
**Manchester United**
*(England)*
**169 million** fans

**4**
**Paris Saint-Germain**
*(France)*
**143 million** fans

**5**
**Juventus**
*(Italy)*
**115 million** fans

## How old are soccer fans?

The chart shows the **percentage** of all soccer fans in five different age groups.

| 16–24 | 25–34 | 35–44 | 45–54 | 55–64 |
|---|---|---|---|---|
| 20% | 28% | 20% | 18% | 13% |

**77** percent of European fans have **traveled abroad** to watch a game. **England** is the most **popular country** for fans to visit to watch a soccer game, followed by **Spain**.

A study of **Europe's top 20 teams** over a period of **seven seasons** revealed that **eight injuries occur** for **every 1,000 hours** of game time.

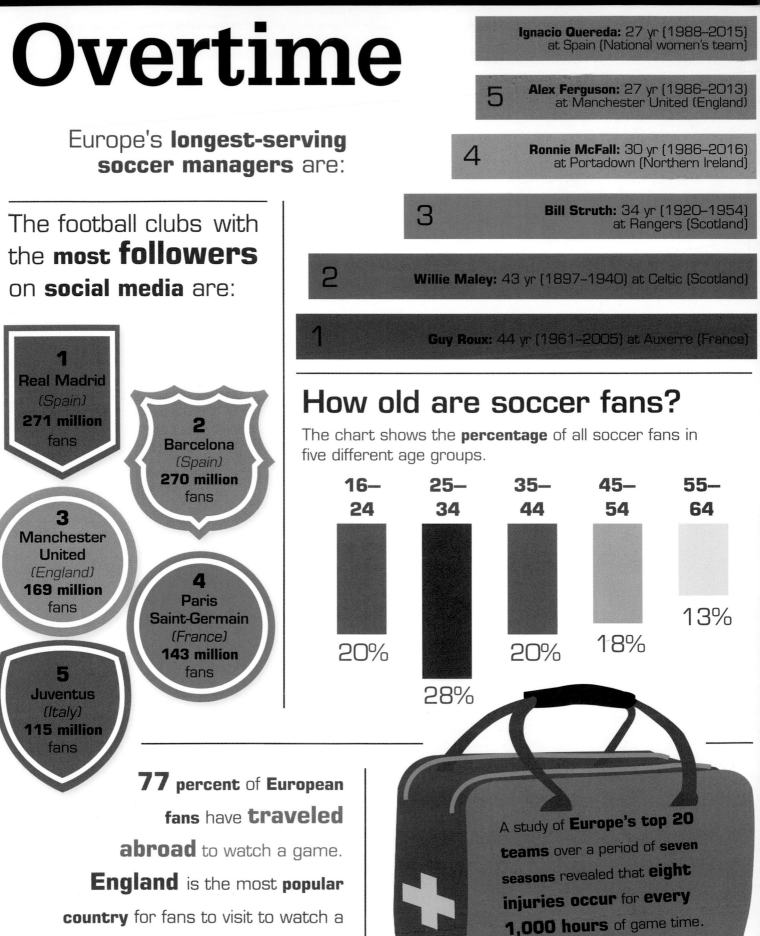

## The **women's matches** with the **highest-ever attendances** were:

**UK, 2012 Olympics**

**1**

**USA vs. Japan**
**80,203** spectators

**UK, 2019**

**2**

**England vs. Germany**
**77,768** spectators

**Spain, 2019**

**3**

**Atletico Madrid vs. Barcelona**
**60,739** spectators

**France, 2019 World Cup**

**4**

**USA vs Netherlands**
**57,900** spectators

**Canada, 2015 World Cup**

**5**

**USA vs. Japan**
**53,341** spectators

---

The **1950 FIFA** World Cup game between **Uruguay and Brazil** at the **Maracanã Stadium** recorded the **highest-ever** attendance:

199,854.

**49%**
North America

The figure refers to the percentage of players in the continent's top leagues who are foreign.

**48%**
Europe

**18%**
Asia

**10%**
Africa

**13.6%**
South America

## **Foreign players** in high demand

Almost half of the professional players signed to the top clubs in **North America** and **Europe** are foreign. These clubs are among the richest and attract the world's best players.

# Tournaments and trophies

The success of a team is measured by the number of tournaments and trophies it has won. At international level, national teams play for the FIFA World Cup every four years. In addition, every continent has its own competition to determine its continental champion.

# FIFA World Cup

Played for the first time in 1930, and staged every four years, the FIFA World Cup is the **biggest competition** in soccer. It decides who becomes the game's **world champion** team.

**Diego Maradona confirmed his status as the world's best player** when he led Argentina to a 3–2 victory over West Germany in the 1986 FIFA World Cup final in the Azteca Stadium, Mexico City.

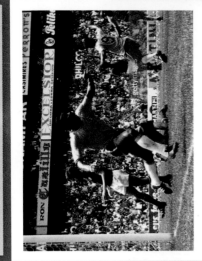

**1970: Brilliant Brazil**
Brazil beat Italy 4–1 in the final in Mexico City. This was the first time two former champions had met in the final. It was also the first time a FIFA World Cup tournament was screened in color.

**2018: Fabulous France**
Kylian Mbappé (center) scored the final goal when France beat Croatia 4–2 in the FIFA World Cup 2018 final, in Moscow, Russia—winning the cup for the second time.

Only 13 teams contested the first FIFA World Cup in Uruguay in 1930.

## COMPETITION FACTS

**First played:**
1930

**Confederation:**
FIFA

**Number of teams:**
32

Qualifying to determine the 32-team line-up for the FIFA World Cup usually starts three years before the start of the tournament.

# UEFA European Championship

The UEFA European Championship was **first played in 1960** and is staged every four years. It determines the **champion of Europe**.

**Italy's captain Giorgio Chiellini** holds the 2020 trophy aloft—the tournament was delayed until 2021 due to the COVID-19 pandemic. The final, against England at Wembley, was decided after Italy won a tense penalty shoot-out 3–2.

## 📊 COMPETITION FACTS

**First played:**
1960

**Confederation:**
UEFA

**Number of teams:**
24

The number of qualifying teams for the UEFA European Championship finals was increased to 24 for the first time in 2016.

Spain and Germany have both won the tournament on three occasions.

### 1984: Allez les Bleus

Michel Platini (above) led France to victory on home soil by scoring nine goals in the tournament (a record), including one in France's 2–0 final victory over Spain.

### 1988: Beautiful orange

Goals from Ruud Gullit and Marco van Basten helped the Netherlands beat the Soviet Union 2–0 in the final. This is the Netherlands' only international tournament victory.

### 2012: Spanish double

Two goals in each half saw Spain demolish Italy 4–0 in the final to become the first team in the tournament's history to defend their title successfully.

# Copa América

The Copa América is the **world's oldest** international soccer tournament. First staged in 1916 and **held every four years**, it determines the **champion of South America**.

## COMPETITION FACTS

**First played:** 1916
**Confederation:** CONMEBOL
**Number of teams:** 12

The current format features 12 teams. There is a group stage (three groups of four teams) that is followed by a knockout stage.

In 2021, **Lionel Messi** lifted his first-ever international trophy after Argentina beat Brazil 1–0 in the final. It had been a long 28 years since Argentina last won the tournament.

Brazil and Uruguay have **won** the tournament every time they have been **hosts**.

## TOURNAMENT HIGHLIGHTS

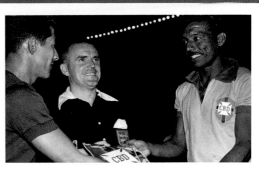

**1949: Brazil end 27-year wait**
Zizinho (above right) led Brazil as they crushed Paraguay 7–0 in the final. It was Brazil's third Copa América success, but the first time they had won the tournament for 27 years.

**1979: Perfect Paraguay**
Paraguay beat Chile 3–1 on aggregate in the final (they won 3–0 in the first leg before losing 1–0 in the second) to win the trophy for the second time.

**1993: Beyond the boundaries**
Argentina beat Mexico 2–1 in the final. This was the first time teams from outside South America (Mexico and the United States) had competed in the tournament.

# Africa Cup of Nations

The **Africa Cup of Nations** is a tournament to decide the **champions of Africa**. It was held for the first time in 1957 and, unlike most other major tournaments, is **staged every two years**.

Only **three countries** took part in the **first-ever Africa Cup of Nations in 1957**.

## 📊 COMPETITION FACTS

**First played:**
1957

**Confederation:**
CAF

**Number of teams:**
24

Qualifying for the tournament sees 48 teams split into 12 groups. The winners and runners-up of each group qualify.

**Kalidou Koulibaly** became the first Senegalese player ever to lift the trophy after his team beat Egypt in the 2022 final. With the game still goalless after extra time, the decisive penalty in the shoot-out was scored by Sadio Mané.

## TOURNAMENT HIGHLIGHTS

### 1988: Classy Cameroon
Cameroon, led by Roger Milla (above), confirmed their status as Africa's dominant team when they beat Nigeria 1–0 in the final. It was their second title in four years.

### 1996: Home comforts
Two goals from Mark Williams saw South Africa mark their first appearance in the tournament by beating Tunisia 2–0 in the final in Johannesburg.

### 2008: Egypt's sensational six
Egypt beat Cameroon 1–0 in the final to win the tournament for the sixth time—a seventh tournament victory followed in 2010.

# AFC Asian Cup

First contested in 1956, the **AFC Asian Cup** is the **second oldest** continental soccer championship in the world, after the Copa América. It is **staged every four years.**

Although outside Asia, **Australia** joined the **AFC** in 2006 and **won the tournament** in 2015.

Qatar beat Japan 3–1 in the 2019 final held in the United Arab Emirates. This was the first time Qatar had won the AFC Asian Cup and the first time Japan had lost a final.

## COMPETITION FACTS

**First played:**
1956

**Confederation:**
AFC

**Number of teams:**
24

Ten teams from five qualifying groups join the teams that finished first, second, and third in the previous tournament, plus the hosts.

## TOURNAMENT HIGHLIGHTS

**1996: Super Saudi**
Goalkeeper Mohamed Al-Deayea (above) helped Saudi Arabia beat the United Arab Emirates 4–2 on penalties in the final, to win the tournament for the third time.

**2007: Jakarta joy for Iraq**
Iraq put the political turmoil in their own country to one side when they beat Saudi Arabia 1–0 in the final in Jakarta, Indonesia, to win the tournament for the first time.

**2011: Fourth title for Japan**
A 109th-minute goal from Tadanari Lee saw Japan beat Australia 1–0 in the final in Doha, Qatar, to win the AFC Asian Cup for a record fourth time.

# Olympic Games

**Men's soccer** was included on the Olympic Games program for the **first time in 1900**. **Women** had to wait until **1996** before they had their own tournament.

## 📈 COMPETITION FACTS

**First played:**
1900 (men);
1996 (women)

**Number of teams:**
16 (men);
12 (women)

The winners of continental age-group tournaments qualify for the men's competition. Women's teams qualify via numerous continental qualifying tournaments.

**Brazil had to wait** an extra year to defend their Olympic title, as the 2020 Tokyo Games were delayed until 2021 by the COVID-19 pandemic. Brazil were victorious over Spain after a 2–1 win in extra time.

Soccer has been played at every summer Olympic Games except 1896 and 1932.

## TOURNAMENT HIGHLIGHTS

### 1952: Mighty Magyars
Hungary, known as the Mighty Magyars, confirmed their status as the best team in world soccer when they beat Yugoslavia 2–0 in the final in Helsinki, Finland.

### 1996: Olympic firsts
The United States won the inaugural women's tournament at the Olympic Games. Nigeria became the first team from Africa to win men's Olympic gold.

### 2020: Canada strikes gold
Canada's women won their first-ever Olympic title by defeating Sweden. After extra time failed to break the 1–1 deadlock, Canada won the penalty shoot-out 3–2.

# FIFA Women's
# World Cup

An unofficial **Women's World Cup**, won by Denmark, was held in Italy in **1970**.

---

## 📈 COMPETITION FACTS

**First played:** 1991
**Confederation:** FIFA
**Number of teams:** 24

Qualifying tournaments are staged in each confederation to determine the 24 teams that qualify for the Women's FIFA World Cup finals.

The **FIFA Women's World Cup** was held for the **first time in 1991**. A 24-team competition, it is **staged every four years**, and is growing in size, recognition, and status.

Alex Morgan lifts the trophy with her United States teammates after beating the Netherlands 2–0 in the 2019 final—a record fourth win for the US. Her teammate Megan Rapinoe (number 15, above right) was awarded the Golden Ball for player of the tournament.

## TOURNAMENT HIGHLIGHTS

**1991: First champions**
Two goals from Michelle Akers saw the United States beat Norway 2–1 to win the first-ever FIFA Women's World Cup final, staged in Guangzhou, China.

**2007: Two in a row**
Germany became the first team to defend their world crown as goals from Birgit Prinz and Simone Laudehr helped them to a 2–0 victory over Brazil in the final.

**2011: Japan's joy**
Japan became the first world champion team from Asia after they beat the United States 3–1 on penalties in the final in Frankfurt, Germany.

## TOURNAMENT HIGHLIGHTS

### 1960: Magnificent Madrid

Alfredo Di Stéfano (three goals) and Ferenc Puskás (two) starred as Real Madrid beat Eintracht Frankfurt 7–3 in the final to record a fifth-successive triumph.

### 1973: Dutch masters

Ajax beat Juventus 1–0 in the final in Belgrade, Serbia, to become the first team since Real Madrid to win three finals in a row.

### 2018: Record-breaking Ronaldo

Real Madrid have won the UEFA Champions League a record 13 times, most recently in 2018. Cristiano Ronaldo (above) is the competition's all-time top scorer.

In 2021, Chelsea clinched their second Champions League title, beating Manchester City in an all-Premier-League final. Midfielder Kai Havertz scored the only goal in a high-quality, competitive match.

A record 380 million viewers tuned in to watch the 2017–18 final on television.

# UEFA Champions **League**

**First staged in 1956** and known as the European Cup until 1992, the UEFA Champions League is considered the world's **most important club competition.**

## 📊 COMPETITION FACTS

**First played:** 1956
**Confederation:** UEFA
**Number of teams:** 78

The top teams from UEFA-qualified countries' domestic leagues qualify for the tournament. The main tournament comprises a 32-team group stage followed by a knockout phase.

# Copa Libertadores

Staged for the first time in 1960 and contested annually, the **Copa Libertadores** is a competition to decide the **top club of South America**.

Pelé (right, in white) inspired Brazil's **Santos** to a second successive title when they beat Argentina's Boca Juniors 5–3 on aggregate in the 1963 final.

## COMPETITION FACTS

**First played:**
1960

**Confederation:**
CONMEBOL

**Number of teams:**
47

Teams qualify for the Copa Libertadores by finishing among the top teams in the various domestic competitions held around South America.

## TOURNAMENT HIGHLIGHTS

**1996: River Plate at the double**
River Plate overturned a 1–0 first-leg deficit to beat Colombia's América 2–1 on aggregate in the final. It was their second title.

**2005: Battle of Brazil**
São Paulo beat Atlético Paranaense 5–1 on aggregate in the final. This was the first-ever final contested by two teams from Brazil.

**2021: Winning streak**
In an all-Brazilian final that went to extra time, Palmeiras defeated Flamengo 2–1 to lift the trophy for the second year running.

Argentine **Carlos Bianchi** is the only manager to **win** the trophy **four times**.

# Roll of honor

## FIFA WORLD CUP

## WINNERS

🏆 **1930:** Uruguay

🏆 **1934:** Italy

🏆 **1938:** Italy

🏆 **1950:** Uruguay

🏆 **1954:** West Germany

🏆 **1958:** Brazil

🏆 **1962:** Brazil

🏆 **1966:** England

🏆 **1970:** Brazil

🏆 **1974:** West Germany

🏆 **1978:** Argentina

🏆 **1982:** Italy

🏆 **1986:** Argentina

🏆 **1990:** West Germany

🏆 **1994:** Brazil

🏆 **1998:** France

🏆 **2002:** Brazil

🏆 **2006:** Italy

🏆 **2010:** Spain

🏆 **2014:** Germany

🏆 **2018:** France

## MOST GOALS SCORED IN A MATCH

### 5—Oleg Salenko
**Russia** v Cameroon, **1994**

## MOST TOURNAMENT WINS

 **Brazil—5**
(1958, 1962, 1970, 1994, 2002)

**Germany—4**
(1954, 1974, 1990, 2014)

**Italy—4**
(1934, 1938, 1982, 2006)

**Uruguay—2**
(1930, 1950)

**Argentina—2**
(1978, 1986)

 **France—2**
(1998, 2018)

 **England—1**
(1966)

**Spain—1**
(2010)

## MOST GOALS SCORED IN A **FINAL**

### 3
### Geoff Hurst

England v West Germany, 1966

## MOST GOALS IN A TOURNAMENT

⚽ **Just Fontaine—13**
(France, 1958)

⚽ **Sándor Kocsis—11**
(Hungary, 1954)

⚽ **Gerd Müller—10**
(West Germany, 1970)

⚽ **Eusebio—9**
(Portugal, 1966)

⚽ **Guillermo Stábile—8**
(Uruguay, 1930)

⚽ **Ronaldo—8**
(Brazil, 2002)

## UEFA EUROPEAN CHAMPIONSHIP

# WINNERS

- 🏆 **1960:** Soviet Union
- 🏆 **1964:** Spain
- 🏆 **1968:** Italy
- 🏆 **1972:** West Germany
- 🏆 **1976:** Czechoslovakia
- 🏆 **1980:** West Germany
- 🏆 **1984:** France
- 🏆 **1988:** Netherlands
- 🏆 **1992:** Denmark
- 🏆 **1996:** Germany
- 🏆 **2000:** France
- 🏆 **2004:** Greece
- 🏆 **2008:** Spain
- 🏆 **2012:** Spain
- 🏆 **2016:** Portugal
- 🏆 **2020:** Italy

## MOST GOALS IN A TOURNAMENT

- ⚽ **9—Michel Platini** (France, 1984)
- ⚽ **6—Antoine Griezmann** (France, 2016)
- ⚽ **5—Marco van Basten** (Netherlands, 1988)

  **Alan Shearer** (England, 1996)

  **Patrick Kluivert** (Netherlands, 2000)

  **Savo Milosevic** (Yugoslavia, 2000)

  **Milan Baroš** (Czech Republic, 2004)

  **Cristiano Ronaldo** (Portugal, 2020)

  **Patrik Schick** (Czech Republic 2020)

**Portugal** won the **first UEFA Nations League final in 2019**—a competition in which all **55 UEFA members** compete.

## COPA AMÉRICA

# WINNERS

- 🏆 **1916:** Uruguay
- 🏆 **1917:** Uruguay
- 🏆 **1919:** Brazil
- 🏆 **1920:** Uruguay
- 🏆 **1921:** Argentina
- 🏆 **1922:** Brazil
- 🏆 **1923:** Uruguay
- 🏆 **1924:** Uruguay
- 🏆 **1925:** Argentina
- 🏆 **1926:** Uruguay
- 🏆 **1927:** Argentina
- 🏆 **1929:** Argentina
- 🏆 **1935:** Uruguay
- 🏆 **1937:** Argentina
- 🏆 **1939:** Peru
- 🏆 **1941:** Argentina
- 🏆 **1942:** Uruguay
- 🏆 **1945:** Argentina
- 🏆 **1946:** Argentina
- 🏆 **1947:** Argentina
- 🏆 **1949:** Brazil
- 🏆 **1953:** Paraguay
- 🏆 **1955:** Argentina
- 🏆 **1956:** Uruguay
- 🏆 **1957:** Argentina
- 🏆 **1959:** Argentina
- 🏆 **1959:** Uruguay*
- 🏆 **1963:** Bolivia
- 🏆 **1967:** Uruguay
- 🏆 **1975:** Peru
- 🏆 **1979:** Paraguay
- 🏆 **1983:** Uruguay
- 🏆 **1987:** Uruguay
- 🏆 **1989:** Brazil
- 🏆 **1991:** Argentina
- 🏆 **1993:** Argentina
- 🏆 **1995:** Uruguay
- 🏆 **1997:** Brazil
- 🏆 **1999:** Brazil
- 🏆 **2001:** Colombia
- 🏆 **2004:** Brazil
- 🏆 **2007:** Brazil
- 🏆 **2011:** Uruguay
- 🏆 **2015:** Chile
- 🏆 **2016:** Chile
- 🏆 **2019:** Brazil
- 🏆 **2021:** Argentina

*An extra tournament was held in 1959*

## MOST WINS
### AS A MANAGER

# 6

**Guillermo Stábile**
**(Argentina)**
**1941, 1945, 1946, 1947, 1955, 1957**

## MOST TOURNAMENT
# WINS

**Uruguay**
15

**Argentina**
15

**Brazil**
9

## AFRICA CUP OF NATIONS

# WINNERS

- 1957: Egypt
- 1959: Egypt
- 1962: Ethiopia
- 1963: Ghana
- 1965: Ghana
- 1968: Congo-Kinshasa
- 1970: Sudan
- 1972: Congo
- 1974: Zaire
- 1976: Morocco
- 1978: Ghana
- 1980: Nigeria
- 1982: Ghana
- 1984: Cameroon
- 1986: Egypt
- 1988: Cameroon
- 1990: Algeria
- 1992: Ivory Coast
- 1994: Nigeria
- 1996: South Africa
- 1998: Egypt
- 2000: Cameroon
- 2002: Cameroon
- 2004: Tunisia
- 2006: Egypt
- 2008: Egypt
- 2010: Egypt
- 2012: Zambia
- 2013: Nigeria
- 2015: Ivory Coast
- 2017: Cameroon
- 2019: Algeria
- 2022: Senegal

## MOST GOALS IN A TOURNAMENT

- **Ndaye Mulamba – 9** (Zaire, 1974)
- **Laurent Pokou – 8** (Ivory Coast, 1970)
- **Benny McCarthy – 7** (South Africa, 1998)
- **Vincent Aboubakar – 8** (Cameroon, 2022)
- **Hossam Hassan – 7** (Egypt, 1998)
- **Laurent Pokou – 6** (Ivory Coast, 1968)

## AFC ASIAN CUP

# WINNERS

- 1956: South Korea
- 1960: South Korea
- 1964: Israel
- 1968: Iran
- 1972: Iran
- 1976: Iran
- 1980: Kuwait
- 1984: Saudi Arabia
- 1988: Saudi Arabia
- 1992: Japan
- 1996: Saudi Arabia
- 2000: Japan
- 2004: Japan
- 2007: Iraq
- 2011: Japan
- 2015: Australia
- 2019: Qatar

## MOST TOURNAMENT WINS

**Japan** 4

**Iran** 3

**Saudi Arabia** 3

## OLYMPIC GAMES

# WINNERS

- 🏆 **1900:** Great Britain
- 🏆 **1904:** Canada
- 🏆 **1908:** Great Britain
- 🏆 **1912:** Great Britain
- 🏆 **1920:** Belgium
- 🏆 **1924:** Uruguay
- 🏆 **1928:** Uruguay
- 🏆 **1932:** *No tournament*
- 🏆 **1936:** Italy
- 🏆 **1948:** Sweden
- 🏆 **1952:** Hungary
- 🏆 **1956:** Soviet Union
- 🏆 **1960:** Yugoslavia
- 🏆 **1964:** Hungary
- 🏆 **1968:** Hungary
- 🏆 **1972:** Poland
- 🏆 **1976:** East Germany
- 🏆 **1980:** Czechoslovakia
- 🏆 **1984:** France
- 🏆 **1988:** Soviet Union
- 🏆 **1992:** Spain
- 🏆 **1996:** Nigeria (men); United States (women)
- 🏆 **2000:** Cameroon (men); Norway (women)
- 🏆 **2004:** Argentina (men); United States (women)
- 🏆 **2008:** Argentina (men); United States (women)
- 🏆 **2012:** Mexico (men); United States (women)
- 🏆 **2016:** Brazil (men); Germany (women)
- 🏆 **2020:** Brazil (men); Canada (women)

## WOMEN: MOST TOURNAMENT WINS

- United States 4
- Norway 1
- Germany 1
- Canada 1

## MEN: MOST TOURNAMENT WINS

- Great Britain 3
- Hungary 3
- Argentina 2
- Soviet Union 2
- Brazil 2

## WOMEN: MOST GOALS IN A TOURNAMENT

- ⚽ **Vivianne Miedema – 10** (Netherlands, 2020)
- ⚽ **Christine Sinclair – 6** (Canada, 2012)
- ⚽ **Barbara Banda – 6** (Zambia, 2020)
- ⚽ **Ellen White – 6** (GB, 2020)
- ⚽ **Sam Kerr – 6** (Australia, 2020)

## FIFA WOMEN'S WORLD CUP

# WINNERS

- 🏆 **1991:** United States
- 🏆 **1995:** Norway
- 🏆 **1999:** United States
- 🏆 **2003:** Germany
- 🏆 **2007:** Germany
- 🏆 **2011:** Japan
- 🏆 **2015:** United States
- 🏆 **2019:** United States

## MOST GOALS IN A TOURNAMENT

- ⚽ **Michelle Akers—10** (United States, 1991)
- ⚽ **Heidi Mohr—7** (Germany, 1991)
- ⚽ **Sissi—7** (Brazil, 1999)
- ⚽ **Sun Wen—7** (China, 1999)
- ⚽ **Birgit Prinz—7** (Germany, 2003)

## MOST TOURNAMENT WINS

- United States 4
- Germany 2
- Norway 1
- Japan 1

**Carli Lloyd** of the **United States** scored the fastest ever **hat-trick** in a final at the **2015 Women's World Cup** against Japan.

## UEFA CHAMPIONS LEAGUE

# WINNERS

🏆 **1956**: Real Madrid
🏆 **1957**: Real Madrid
🏆 **1958**: Real Madrid
🏆 **1959**: Real Madrid
🏆 **1960**: Real Madrid
🏆 **1961**: Benfica
🏆 **1962**: Benfica
🏆 **1963**: Milan
🏆 **1964**: Internazionale
🏆 **1965**: Internazionale
🏆 **1966**: Real Madrid
🏆 **1967**: Celtic
🏆 **1968**: Manchester United
🏆 **1969**: Milan
🏆 **1970**: Feyenoord
🏆 **1971**: Ajax
🏆 **1972**: Ajax
🏆 **1973**: Ajax
🏆 **1974**: Bayern Munich
🏆 **1975**: Bayern Munich
🏆 **1976**: Bayern Munich
🏆 **1977**: Liverpool
🏆 **1978**: Liverpool

🏆 **1979**: Nottingham Forest
🏆 **1980**: Nottingham Forest
🏆 **1981**: Liverpool
🏆 **1982**: Aston Villa
🏆 **1983**: Hamburg
🏆 **1984**: Liverpool
🏆 **1985**: Juventus
🏆 **1986**: Steaua Bucharest
🏆 **1987**: Porto
🏆 **1988**: PSV Eindhoven
🏆 **1989**: Milan
🏆 **1990**: Milan
🏆 **1991**: Red Star Belgrade
🏆 **1992**: Barcelona
🏆 **1993**: Marseille
🏆 **1994**: Milan
🏆 **1995**: Ajax
🏆 **1996**: Juventus
🏆 **1997**: Borussia Dortmund
🏆 **1998**: Real Madrid

🏆 **1999**: Manchester United
🏆 **2000**: Real Madrid
🏆 **2001**: Bayern Munich
🏆 **2002**: Real Madrid
🏆 **2003**: Milan
🏆 **2004**: Porto
🏆 **2005**: Liverpool
🏆 **2006**: Barcelona
🏆 **2007**: Milan
🏆 **2008**: Manchester United
🏆 **2009**: Barcelona
🏆 **2010**: Internazionale
🏆 **2011**: Barcelona
🏆 **2012**: Chelsea
🏆 **2013**: Bayern Munich
🏆 **2014**: Real Madrid
🏆 **2015**: Barcelona
🏆 **2016**: Real Madrid
🏆 **2017**: Real Madrid
🏆 **2018**: Real Madrid
🏆 **2019**: Liverpool
🏆 **2020**: Bayern Munich
🏆 **2021**: Chelsea

## MOST GOALS IN A TOURNAMENT

⚽ **Cristiano Ronaldo—17**
(Real Madrid, Spain 2013–14)

⚽ **Cristiano Ronaldo—16**
(Real Madrid, Spain 2015–16)

⚽ **Cristiano Ronaldo—15**
(Real Madrid, Spain 2017–18)

 **Robert Lewandowski—15**
(Bayern Munich, Germany 2019–20)

⚽ **Jose Altafini—14**
(Milan, Italy 1962–63)

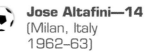 **Lionel Messi—14**
(Barcelona, Spain 2011–12)

 **Ferenc Puskás—12**
(Real Madrid, Spain 1959–60)

⚽ **Gerd Müller—12**
(Bayern Munich, Germany 1972–73)

⚽ **Ruud van Nistelrooy—12**
(Manchester United, England 2002–03)

⚽ **Lionel Messi—12**
(Barcelona, Spain 2010–11 and 2018–19)

 **Cristiano Ronaldo—12**
(Real Madrid, Spain 2016–17)

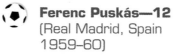

## COPA LIBERTADORES

# WINNERS

🏆 **1960**: Peñarol
🏆 **1961**: Peñarol
🏆 **1962**: Santos
🏆 **1963**: Santos
🏆 **1964**: Independiente
🏆 **1965**: Independiente
🏆 **1966**: Peñarol
🏆 **1967**: Racing
🏆 **1968**: Estudiantes
🏆 **1969**: Estudiantes
🏆 **1970**: Estudiantes
🏆 **1971**: Nacional
🏆 **1972**: Independiente
🏆 **1973**: Independiente
🏆 **1974**: Independiente
🏆 **1975**: Independiente
🏆 **1976**: Cruzeiro
🏆 **1977**: Boca Juniors
🏆 **1978**: Boca Juniors
🏆 **1979**: Olimpia
🏆 **1980**: Nacional

🏆 **1981**: Flamengo
🏆 **1982**: Peñarol
🏆 **1983**: Grêmio
🏆 **1984**: Independiente
🏆 **1985**: Argentinos Juniors
🏆 **1986**: River Plate
🏆 **1987**: Peñarol
🏆 **1988**: Nacional
🏆 **1989**: Atlético Nacional
🏆 **1990**: Olimpia
🏆 **1991**: Colo-Colo
🏆 **1992**: São Paulo
🏆 **1993**: São Paulo
🏆 **1994**: Vélez Sársfield
🏆 **1995**: Grêmio
🏆 **1996**: River Plate
🏆 **1997**: Cruzeiro
🏆 **1998**: Vasco da Gama
🏆 **1999**: Palmeiras
🏆 **2000**: Boca Juniors
🏆 **2001**: Boca Juniors
🏆 **2002**: Olimpia

🏆 **2003**: Boca Juniors
🏆 **2004**: Once Caldas
🏆 **2005**: São Paulo
🏆 **2006**: Internacional
🏆 **2007**: Boca Juniors
🏆 **2008**: LDU Quito
🏆 **2009**: Estudiantes
🏆 **2010**: Internacional
🏆 **2011**: Santos
🏆 **2012**: Corinthians
🏆 **2013**: Atlético Mineiro
🏆 **2014**: San Lorenzo
🏆 **2015**: River Plate
🏆 **2016**: Atlético Nacional
🏆 **2017**: Grêmio
🏆 **2018**: River Plate
🏆 **2019**: Flamengo
🏆 **2020**: Palmeiras
🏆 **2021**: Palmeiras

# MOST GOALS IN A TOURNAMENT

⚽ **Daniel Onega—17**
(River Plate, Argentina—1966)

⚽ **Luizão—15**
(Corinthians, Brazil—2000)

⚽ **Norberto Raffo—14**
(Racing, Argentina—1967)

⚽ **Palhinha—13**
(Cruzeiro, Brazil—1976)

⚽ **Mário Jardel—12**
(Grêmio, Brazil—1995)

# MOST WINS BY COUNTRY:

| | | |
|---|---|---|
| 🏴 | 25 | Argentina |
| 🏴 | 21 | Brazil |
| 🏴 | 8 | Uruguay |
| 🏴 | 3 | Colombia |
| 🏴 | 3 | Paraguay |
| 🏴 | 1 | Chile |
| 🏴 | 1 | Ecuador |

# MOST TOURNAMENT WINS

**Independiente**
(Argentina)—**7**

**Boca Juniors**
(Argentina)—**6**

**Peñarol**
(Uruguay)—**5**

**Estudiantes**
(Argentina)—**4**

**River Plate**
(Argentina)—**4**

# GLOSSARY

Here are the meanings of some words relating to soccer rules, tactics, and equipment.

## Added time
The amount of time added at the end of each half to make up for stoppages during the game.

## Assist
A pass in a game that directly leads to a goal.

## Attacking team
The team that is in possession of the ball.

## Away game
A game that is played in the opponent's stadium.

## Back four
The four players in front of the goalkeeper who form the defensive line.

## Bench
The area next to the field in which the team staff and substitutes sit during a game.

## Box-to-box midfielder
A midfielder who plays in both attack and defense, moving from one penalty box to the other.

## Byline
The markings along the edge of the field between the goalposts and corner flags.

## Caution
When the referee shows a player a yellow card for a serious offense.

## Center circle
The circular marking in the middle of the field.

## Center spot
The mark in the middle of the field, where the ball is placed during kick off.

## Clean sheet
Describes a result in which a team does not concede a goal in a game.

## Clearance
A defensive move in which a player kicks the ball away from goal.

## Corner arc
The white arc at each corner of the field from which corners are taken.

## Cross
A ball kicked from the side of the field, aimed at a teammate in or near the penalty area.

## Far post
The goalpost farthest from where the ball is in play.

## First touch
The first contact a player makes with the ball to control it.

## Formation
The arrangement of the different players on a field—the formation dictates whether a team plays in an attacking or defensive style.

## Goal kick
The method of restarting play when the ball has crossed the goal line when last touched by an attacking player.

## Goal line
The line marking between the goal posts; a goal is awarded when the whole ball crosses the goal line.

## Handball
An infringement in which a player (other than the goalkeeper) touches the ball with the hand or arm.

## Halftime
The 15-minute rest period between the first and second halves.

## Hat trick
Describes the feat of a player who scores three goals in a single game.

## Injury time
The time added at the end of each half to make up for time lost to injuries, fouls, substitutions, and other incidents.

## Kickoff
The method of starting a game, or restarting play after a goal. Two teammates place the ball on the center spot and kick the ball into play.

## Near post
The goalpost closest to where the ball is in play.

## Offside trap
A move in which the back four step forward together in an attempt to put the opposition into an offside position.

## One-on-one marking
A method of defending set pieces in which each defender is responsible for watching a specific attacker.

## Overtime
The two additional 15-minute periods played in cup tournaments when the score is still tied after 90 minutes.

## Own goal
When a player scores against their own team, usually through an accidental deflection.

## Penalty shoot-out
A method of deciding a winner when scores are still level after overtime.

## Playmaker
A player, typically a midfielder, who controls the team's attacking flow.

## Professional foul
A foul deliberately committed to stop the opponent from scoring.

## Sending off
A situation in which the referee shows a red card to a player, who must leave the playing field immediately.

## Set piece
Refers to the method—either a throw-in, corner, or free kick—used to restart play after an infringement or after the ball has gone out of play.

## Substitution
The changing of players during the course of a game. In competitive matches, a team can make up to three substitutions.

## Sweeper
An extra defensive player who helps the back four by dealing with any defensive errors.

## Technical area
The area outside the touchline from which managers shout instructions to the team during a game.

## Throw-in
The method of restarting play when the ball goes over the touchline. It involves throwing the ball back in play while keeping both feet on or outside the touchline.

## Touchline
The marking along each side of the field that denotes the edge of the playing field.

## Wall
The lineup of defenders during a direct free kick, who try to limit the shooting angle of the free-kick taker.

## Zonal marking
A defensive system of play in which players are given a specific area to guard.

# INDEX

Page numbers in **bold** refer to main entries

# ACKNOWLEDGMENTS

Dorling Kindersley would like to thank Carron Brown for the index, Anna Limerick for proofreading, and Nick McCabe for additional advice.

The publisher would like to thank the following for their kind permission to reproduce their photographs:

(Key: a-above; b-below/bottom; c-center; f-far; l-left; r-right; t-top)

1 Getty Images: Dmytro Aksonov (cb). 2 Dreamstime.com: Tom Wang (tr). Getty Images: Dmytro Aksonov (cr). 3 Alamy Stock Photo: Fredrick Kippe (tc). Getty Images: Dmytro Aksonov (cla); Dmytro Aksonov (bl); Dmytro Aksonov (c); Peter Read Miller / Contributor (tr). 4-5 Dreamstime.com: Tom Wang. 6-7 Dorling Kindersley: Stuart Jackson-Carter | SJC Illustration. 7 123RF.com: Konstantin Kalishko (tl). 8-9 Bridgeman Images: National Football Museum, Manchester, UK. 9 National Football Museum: (tr). 10 123RF.com: alhovik (tr); Richard Thomas (clb). Getty Images: Hulton Archive / Stringer (tl). 10-11 123RF.com: Andrey Kryuchkov (cb). 11 123RF.com: alhovik (clb/ball, crb/ball); Andriy Popov (crb). iStockphoto.com: 4x6 (clb). 12-13 Getty Images: Dmytro Aksonov. 14 Mary Evans Picture Library: Illustrated London News Ltd (tl). 14-15 Rex Shutterstock: Xinhua News Agency. 16 123RF.com: Gordana Damjanovic (clb); yukipon (cb); Christos Georghiou (crb). 18-19 Getty Images: Dmytro Aksonov. 20 Getty Images: Popperfoto (cr). iStockphoto.com: Arkhom1983 (cb). Mary Evans Picture Library: (bc). 20-21 Getty Images: David Price (b). 21 Getty Images: Imagno (ca); Popperfoto (cl, cb, bc). 22-23 KJA-Artists: Jon@KJA-Artists. 23 Pitch Heating Limited: (bc). 24 123RF.com: Olexandr Moroz / alexandrmoroz (cra). SWNS.com Ltd: (bl). 26-27 KJA-Artists: Jon@KJA-artists. 28-29 Nike: (c). 29 iStockphoto.com: richjem (tr). 30-31 KJA-Artists: Jon@KJA-artists. 30 Getty Images: Ian Kington (bc); Visionhaus (cla). 31 Getty Images: Dean Mouhtaropoulos (bc); Jean-Sebastien Evrard / AFP (c). 32-33 Getty Images: Dmytro Aksonov (background); Matthew Ashton (t). 32 Getty Images: NurPhoto (crb). 34-35 123RF.com: Monika Mlynek

(Stadium). Fotolia: Fotoedgaras (Stopwatch). Getty Images: Bernhard Lang. 34 Getty Images: Helios de la Rubia (tl). iStockphoto.com: jamielawton (tc); PeopleImages (tr). 35 Getty Images: Gallo Images - Robbert Koene (tc); Alex Grimm / Bongarts (tr). Rex Shutterstock: Friedmann Vogel (tl). 36 Getty Images: Ben Radford (clb). 38-39 Getty Images: Dmytro Aksonov. 40-41 Rex Shutterstock: Image Source. 41 Rex Shutterstock: Matthew Impey / Wired Photos (crb). 42 Alamy Stock Photo: Reuters (clb). Dreamstime.com: Tungphoto (c). 44-45 Getty Images: Jamie Squire / Staff / Getty Images Sport. 46-47 Getty Images: Dmytro Aksonov / E+. 46 123RF.com: Ogm (bl). 48-49 Photo courtesy GoalControl GmbH. 49 Getty Images: Cameron Spencer / Staff (tr). 50 Catapult: (tl). Dorling Kindersley: Jon@KJA-Artists (tr). 54-55 iStockphoto.com: E+ / Lorado. 56-57 Getty Images: Dmytro Aksonov. 57 Getty Images: Dmytro Aksonov (baclground). 58 Getty Images: Dmytro Aksonov (c). 58-59 Getty Images: Dmytro Aksonov. 59 Getty Images: Dani Pozo / Stringer / AFP (bc); Dmytro Aksonov (cr); Dmytro Aksonov (cl). 60 Getty Images: Jean-Yves Ruszniewski / Contributor (clb). 60-61 Getty Images: Dmytro Aksonov. 62-63 Getty Images: Dmytro Aksonov; Dmytro Aksonov (taking the kick). 63 Getty Images: Popperfoto / Contributor (bc). 64-65 Getty Images: Dmytro Aksonov (Background); Dmytro Aksonov (c). 64 Getty Images: Matthias Hangst / Staff (clb). 66-67 Getty Images: Dmytro Aksonov (Background); Dmytro Aksonov (c). 66 Getty Images: Pedro Ugarte / Staff / AFP (cl). 68-69 Getty Images: Dmytro Aksonov (Background); Dmytro Aksonov (b). 72-73 Alamy Stock Photo: Fredrick Kippe. 74-75 Getty Images: Dmytro Aksonov. 74 Getty Images: Drew Hallowell / Stringer (cl). 77 Getty Images: Ullstein Bild / Contributor (tr). 79 Getty Images: STF / Staff / AFP (br). 81 Press Association Images: (tr). 82-83 123RF.com: Monika Mlynek (background). 84 Getty Images: Rolls Press / Popperfoto / Contributor (bc). 84-85 123RF.com: Monika Mlynek. 88-89 123RF.com: Monika Mlynek. 90 Getty Images: Popperfoto / Contributor (tc);

Popperfoto / Contributor (cla); Mondadori Portfolio / Contributor (cra); Popperfoto / Contributor (br). 91 Dorling Kindersley: Adam Brackenbury / Stefan Podhorodecki (r). Getty Images: Matthew Ashton - AMA / Contributor (tl); Jasper Juinen / Staff (ca); Popperfoto / Contributor (clb); VI-Images / Contributor (bl); VI-Images / Contributor (cb). 93 Dreamstime.com: Connie Larsen (br). 94-95 Getty Images: Dmytro Aksonov. 98-99 KJA-Artists: Jon@KJA-Artists. 100-101 Allianz: (ca/all images). 102 Dreamstime.com: Dmitry Rukhlenko (cb). Getty Images: Gary Burchell (crb); Yosuke Tanaka / Aflo (l). 102-103 123RF.com: Andrey Kryuchkov (b). 103 Dreamstime.com: Berean (clb). Getty Images: Creative Crop / Digital Vision (cb); Yosuke Tanaka / Aflo (r). 104-105 Getty Images: Westend61. 104 Rex Shutterstock: Brad Smith / ISI / REX (br). 105 123RF.com: Burak Cakmak (br); Wavebreak Media Ltd (bc). Getty Images: Steve Bardens-FIFA / Contributor / FIFA (tr). Rex Shutterstock: John Dorton / ISI / REX (bl). 106-107 123RF.com: Videodoctor (c). 107 Getty Images: Marcus Brandt / Staff / AFP (br). 108 Getty Images: Stuart MacFarlane / Contributor (clb). 108-109 Dreamstime.com: Libux77 (c). Getty Images: Image Source (b). 110-111 Getty Images: Dmytro Aksonov. 111 Getty Images: Conor Molloy / Contributor (crb). 114-115 Getty Images: Peter Read Miller / Contributor. 116-117 Getty Images: Bob Thomas / Contributor. 116 Getty Images: Popperfoto / Contributor (tl). Getty Images: Jewel Samad (cra). 118-119 Getty Images: Michael Regan / UEFA (main).119 Getty Images: Getty Images / Staff (tr); AFP / Stringer (crb); Professional Sport / Contributor (cr). 120-121 Getty Images: Buda Mendes (main). 121 Getty Images: Tim Clary / Staff / AFP (crb); AFP / Getty Images / Staff (cr); Popperfoto / Contributor (tr). 122-123 Getty Images: Ayman Aref / NurPhoto (main). 123 Getty Images: Gallo Images / Stringer (crb); Mark Thompson / Staff (cr); Bob Thomas / Contributor (tr). 124-125 Getty Images: Zhizhao Wu. 125 Alamy Stock Photo: Reuters (tr). Rex Shutterstock: Jurnasyanto Sukarno / EPA / REX (cr); Stringer / EPA / REX (crb). 126-127 Getty

Images: Anne-Christine Poujoulat / AFP (main). 127 Getty Images: Abbie Parr (br); Bob Thomas / Contributor (cr). TopFoto.co.uk: © 2003 Credit:Topham / PA (tr). 128-129 Alamy Stock Photo: Xinhua. 129 Getty Images: Tommy Cheng / Staff (tr); Paul Gilham / Staff (cr). Rex Shutterstock: Imago / Back Page Images / REX (crb). 130-131 Reuters: David Ramos (main). 130 Getty Images: VI-Images / Contributor (cl). Getty Images: Laurence Griffiths (clb). TopFoto.co.uk: © PA Photos (tl). 132-133 Getty Images: Popperfoto / Contributor. 133 Getty Images: Vanderlei Almeida / Staff (cr); Ernesto Ryan (br); Sergio Goya / Stringer (tr). 134-135 Dreamstime.com: Donkeyru. 136-187 Dreamstime.com: Donkeyru. 138-139 Dreamstime.com: Donkeyru. 141 iStockphoto.com: Dmytro Aksonov (br).

All other images © Dorling Kindersley